P9-CDU-087

SPECTRUM®

Math

Grade 6

Free Video Tutorials

On select pages, you will see a QR code for an instructional video that corresponds to the skills.

To access the video from your smartphone or tablet:

- Download a free QR code scanner from your device's app store.
- Launch the scanning app on your device.
- Scan the code, which will bring you to the *Spectrum Math, Grade 6* website.
- Select the video that matches the title from your workbook page.

All videos are also available at carsondellosa.com/math-6 and www.youtube.com/user/CarsonDellosaPub.

Published by Spectrum®
an imprint of Carson-Dellosa Publishing
Greensboro, NC

Spectrum®
An imprint of Carson-Dellosa Publishing LLC
P.O. Box 35665
Greensboro, NC 27425 USA

© 2015 Carson-Dellosa Publishing LLC. Except as permitted under the United States Copyright Act, no part of this publication may be reproduced, stored, or distributed in any form or by any means (mechanically, electronically, recording, etc.) without the prior written consent of Carson-Dellosa Publishing LLC. Spectrum® is an imprint of Carson-Dellosa Publishing LLC.

Printed in the USA • All rights reserved.

ISBN 978-1-4838-0874-1

06-201157811

Table of Contents Grade 6

Table of Contents, continued

Check What You Know

Understanding the Number System and Operations

Rewrite each expression using the Distributive Property.

a

b

1. $4 \times (6 + 2) =$ __24__

$(2 \times 5) + (2 \times 4) =$ __18__ [10 8]

2. $4 \times (2 + 6) =$ __32__

$6 \times (5 - 1) =$ __24__ [6 × 4]

3. $(3 \times 6) - (3 \times 3) =$ __9__ [18 9]

$8 \times (3 - 1) =$ __32__

Find the Greatest Common Factor of each set of numbers.

a   **b**   **c**

4. 15, 20 __5__   12, 36 __6__ 12   72, 60 __12__

5. 65, 39 __13__   95, 76 __19__   96, 112 __16__

Find the Least Common Multiple of each set of numbers.

6. 12, 3 __6/12__   15, 3, 2 __30__   4, 7 __28__

7. 7, 10, 3 __210__   12, 6 __12__   7, 3, 5 __105__

NAME _____

Check What You Know

Understanding the Number System and Operations

Multiply or divide.

	a	**b**	**c**	**d**

8.

a)
```
   3 1 2
 × 2 6 3
```

b)
```
   4 2 8
 × 3 2 1
```

c)
```
   2 1 8 5
 ×   2 1 6
```

d)
```
   3 3 7 2
 ×   3 5 1
```

9.

a) 73)6278

b) 54)8239

c) 27)54702

d) 83)96542

10.

a)
```
   2.8 6
 ×   0.3
```

b)
```
   0.8 2
 × 0.4 3
```

c)
```
  $7 8.5 3
 ×      1 6
```

d)
```
   3.2 1
 × 8.7 2
```

11.

a) 0.08)64

b) 0.3)726

c) 0.83)2.1995

d) 14)$7.70

SHOW YOUR WORK

Solve each problem.

12. One bag of peanuts costs $1.52. How many bags can you buy with $34.96?

You can buy _____ bags.

12.

13. A box containing 78.4 pounds of coffee will be divided into containers that hold 0.56 pounds each. How many containers can be filled?

_____ containers can be filled.

13.

Lesson 1.1   Number Properties

There are certain rules or properties of math that are always true.

The **Commutative Properties** of addition and multiplication state that the order in which numbers are added or multiplied does not change the result.

$a + b = b + a$ and $a \times b = b \times a$
$2 + 3 = 5$ $5 \times 2 = 10$
$3 + 2 = 5$ $2 \times 5 = 10$

The **Associative Properties** of addition and multiplication state that the way in which addends or factors are grouped does not change the result.

$(a + b) + c = a + (b + c)$ and $(a \times b) \times c = a \times (b \times c)$
$(2 + 3) + 4 = 2 + (3 + 4)$ $(2 \times 4) \times 5 = 2 \times (4 \times 5)$
$5 + 4 = 2 + 7$ $8 \times 5 = 2 \times 20$
$9 = 9$ $40 = 40$

The **Identity Property of Addition** states that the sum of an addend and 0 is the addend.
$5 + 0 = 5$

The **Identity Property of Multiplication** states that the product of a factor and 1 is that factor. $4 \times 1 = 4$

The **Properties of Zero** state that the product of a factor and 0 is 0. $5 \times 0 = 0$

The properties of zero also state that the quotient of zero and any non-zero divisor is 0. $0 \div 5 = 0$

Name the property shown by each statement.

	a	**b**
1.	$2 \times 8 = 8 \times 2$ _____	$2 + (3 + 4) = (2 + 3) + 4$ _____
2.	$35 \times 1 = 35$ _____	$32 + 25 = 25 + 32$ _____
3.	$4 \times (6 \times 2) = (4 \times 6) \times 2$ _____	$0 \times 9 = 0$ _____
4.	$45 + 0 = 45$ _____	$18 \times 0 = 0 \times 18$ _____

Rewrite each expression using the property indicated.

5. Associative; $(3 + 5) + 2 =$ _____   Commutative; $5 \times 7 =$ _____

6. Identity; $0 + 4 =$ _____   Associative; $3 \times (2 \times 5) =$ _____

7. Commutative; $7 + 9 =$ _____   Associative; $(2 + 5) + 4 =$ _____

8. Identity; $7 \times 1 =$ _____   Identity; $37 + 0 =$ _____

9. Properties of Zero; $0 \times 12 =$ _____   Properties of Zero; $0 \div 6 =$ _____

Lesson 1.2 The Distributive Property

The **Distributive Property** combines the operations of addition and multiplication.

$$a \times (b + c) \quad = \quad (a \times b) + (a \times c)$$
$$3 \times (2 + 5) \qquad\quad (3 \times 2) + (3 \times 5)$$
$$3 \times 7 \qquad\qquad\quad 6 \;+\; 15$$
$$21 \qquad\qquad\qquad\quad 21$$

Indicate which operation should be done first.

               a   **b**

1. $(2 \times 5) + (2 \times 3)$ _____ $7 \times (3 + 5)$ _____

2. $(6 + 9) \times 4$ _____ $(3 \times 5) + (3 \times 7)$ _____

Rewrite each expression using the Distributive Property.

3. $4 \times (6 + 2) =$ _____ $(2 \times 5) + (2 \times 4) =$ _____

4. $(5 \times 1) + (5 \times 6) =$ _____ $4 \times (2 + 6) =$ _____

5. $8 \times (4 + 3) =$ _____ $(5 \times 0) + (5 \times 1) =$ _____

Write each missing number.

6. $(5 \times 3) + (n \times 4) = 5 \times (3 + 4)$ _____ $7 \times (n + 3) = (7 \times 2) + (7 \times 3)$ _____

7. $n \times (5 + 3) = (6 \times 5) + (6 \times 3)$ _____ $(5 \times 7) + (n \times 4) = 5 \times (7 + 4)$ _____

8. $(4 \times 5) + (4 \times 2) = 4 \times (5 + n)$ _____ $3 \times (n + 5) = (3 \times 4) + (3 \times 5)$ _____

Replace a with 2, b with 5, and c with 3. Then, find the value of each expression

9. $a \times (b + c) =$ _____ $(a \times b) + (a \times c) =$ _____

10. $(c \times a) + (c \times b) =$ _____ $b \times (a + c) =$ _____

Lesson 1.2   The Distributive Property

The **Distributive Property** states: $a \times (b + c) = (a \times b) + (a \times c)$

The same property also means that: $a \times (b - c) = (a \times b) - (a \times c)$

This can help solve complex multiplication problems:

$26 = 20 + 6$ $17 \times 26 = (17 \times 20) + (17 \times 6) = 340 + 102 = 442$

$18 = 20 - 2$ $47 \times 18 = (47 \times 20) - (47 \times 2) = 940 - 94 = 846$

Using the Distributive Property, rewrite each expression in a way that will help solve it. Then, solve.

a   **b**

1. $22 \times 102 =$ _____ = _____ $39 \times 25 =$ _____ = _____

2. $146 \times 33 =$ _____ = _____ $28 \times 16 =$ _____ = _____

3. $36 \times 35 =$ _____ = _____ $51 \times 106 =$ _____ = _____

4. $19 \times 256 =$ _____ = _____ $45 \times 17 =$ _____ = _____

5. $57 \times 38 =$ _____ = _____ $48 \times 45 =$ _____ = _____

6. $82 \times 80 =$ _____ = _____ $51 \times 82 =$ _____ = _____

7. $43 \times 142 =$ _____ = _____ $264 \times 67 =$ _____ = _____

8. $12 \times 39 =$ _____ = _____ $58 \times 35 =$ _____ = _____

Lesson 1.3 Multi-Digit Multiplication

	Multiply 3,263 by 3.	Multiply 3,263 by 40.	Add.
3263 × 43	3263 × 3 ——— 9789	3263 × 40 ——— 130520	3263 × 43 ——— 9789 +130520 ——— 140,309

Multiply.

	a	**b**	**c**	**d**
1.	324 × 27	816 × 16	255 × 44	2165 × 23
2.	5150 × 22	7182 × 12	6324 × 36	4522 × 63
3.	886 ×374	763 ×618	654 ×523	985 ×447
4.	2186 × 342	1898 × 475	3688 × 259	2864 × 723

Lesson 1.4 Multi-Digit Division

983 is between 840 (28 × 30) and 1120 (28 × 40), so the tens digit is 3.

$$
\begin{array}{r}
3 \\
28\overline{)983} \\
-840 \quad \text{subtract}\\
\hline
143
\end{array}
$$

143 is between 140 (28 × 5) and 168 (28 × 6), so the ones digit is 5.

$$
\begin{array}{r}
35\,\text{r}3 \\
28\overline{)983} \\
-840 \quad \text{subtract}\\
\hline
143 \\
-140 \quad \text{subtract}\\
\hline
3 \quad \text{remainder}
\end{array}
$$

Divide.

	a	b	c	d	e
1.	18)94	27)68	22)88	19)78	25)64
2.	43)88	12)84	32)865	24)768	31)913
3.	27)815	54)725	45)880	23)615	18)324

Lesson 1.4 Multi-Digit Division

37,262 is between
32,800 (82 × 400) and
41,000 (82 × 500), so
the hundreds digit is 4.

```
       4
8 2)3 7 2 6 2
 - 3 2 8 0 0   subtract
   ─────────
     4 4 6 2
```

4,462 is between
4,100 (82 × 50) and
4,920 (82 × 60), so the
tens digit is 5.

```
       4 5
8 2)3 7 2 6 2
 - 3 2 8 0 0
   ─────────
     4 4 6 2
   - 4 1 0 0   subtract
     ─────────
       3 6 2
```

362 is between
328 (82 × 4) and
410 (82 × 5), so the
ones digit is 4.

```
       4 5 4 r34
8 2)3 7 2 6 2
 - 3 2 8 0 0
   ─────────
     4 4 6 2
   - 4 1 0 0
     ─────────
       3 6 2
     - 3 2 8   subtract
       ─────────
         3 4   remainder
```

Divide.

	a	b	c	d	e
1.	56)6185	32)9984	27)9984	13)2329	22)2420
2.	45)6950	88)9944	21)5672	78)40794	65)14625
3.	36)52813	63)45675	42)34816	23)20378	18)10242

Lesson 1.5   Reciprocal Operations

Multiplication and division are reciprocal, or opposite, operations. You can use reciprocal operations to check your answers when you work math problems.

$15 \times 4 = 60$ $60 \div 15 = 4$

$8 \times 7 = 56$ $56 \div 8 = 7$

Multiply or divide. Use the reciprocal operation to check your answers.

	a	b	c	d
1.	$\begin{array}{r} 392 \\ \times\ 22 \\ \hline \end{array}$	$\begin{array}{r} 239 \\ \times\ 60 \\ \hline \end{array}$	$\begin{array}{r} 931 \\ \times\ 77 \\ \hline \end{array}$	$\begin{array}{r} 496 \\ \times\ 28 \\ \hline \end{array}$
2.	$\begin{array}{r} 193 \\ \times\ 55 \\ \hline \end{array}$	$\begin{array}{r} 529 \\ \times\ 31 \\ \hline \end{array}$	$\begin{array}{r} 695 \\ \times\ 75 \\ \hline \end{array}$	$\begin{array}{r} 972 \\ \times\ 93 \\ \hline \end{array}$
3.	$21\overline{)2898}$	$22\overline{)7898}$	$71\overline{)5893}$	$32\overline{)4832}$
4.	$11\overline{)3498}$	$33\overline{)5214}$	$42\overline{)4914}$	$12\overline{)8328}$

Lesson 1.6 Problem Solving

SHOW YOUR WORK

Estimate the answers to the following problems. Check your answer by using the opposite operation.

1. There are 527 sixth-grade students who will take a field trip. There are 9 buses. About how many students will be riding in each bus?

   Round 527 to _____.

   About _____ students will ride each bus.

2. At West Side Middle School, there are 42 classrooms with 28 desks in each. About how many desks are there?

   Round 42 to _____ and round 28 to _____.

   There are about _____ desks.

3. There are 563 books to be shelved in the library. Each shelf holds 7 books. About how many shelves will be used?

   Round 563 to _____.

   About _____ shelves will be used.

4. Mrs. Juergen's class is building a model city from craft sticks. Each house requires 267 sticks. The class will build 93 houses. About how many sticks will be needed?

   Round 267 to _____ and round 93 to _____.

   About _____ sticks will be needed.

5. Thirty-eight students are going on a field trip. Parents will drive. Each car can hold 4 students along with the driver. How many cars will be needed?

   Round 38 to _____.

   About _____ cars will be needed.

6. Jorge's family is taking a car trip to see his grandmother. The family plans to spend 3 days on the road. The distance is 687 miles. About how far must they drive each day?

   Round 687 to _____.

   They must drive about _____ miles each day.

1.

2.

3.

4.

5.

6.

Greatest Common Factor

A **factor** is a divisor of a number. (For example, 3 and 4 are both factors of 12.) A **common factor** is a divisor that is shared by two or more numbers (1, 2, 4, and 8). The **greatest common factor** is the largest common factor shared by the numbers (8).

To find the greatest common factor of 32 and 40, list all of the factors of each.

$$32 \begin{cases} 1 \times 32 \\ 2 \times 16 \\ 4 \times 8 \end{cases} \text{1, 2, 4, 8, 16, and 32}$$

$$40 \begin{cases} 1 \times 40 \\ 2 \times 20 \\ 4 \times 10 \\ 5 \times 8 \end{cases} \text{1, 2, 4, 5, 8, 10, 20, and 40}$$

The greatest common factor is 8.

List the factors of each number below. Then, list the common factors and the greatest common factor.

	Factors	**Common Factors**	**Greatest Common Factor**
1. 8	_____	_____	_____
12	_____		
2. 6	_____	_____	_____
18	_____		
3. 24	_____	_____	_____
15	_____		
4. 4	_____	_____	_____
6	_____		
5. 5	_____	_____	_____
12	_____		
6. 16	_____	_____	_____
12	_____		

Lesson 1.7   Greatest Common Factor

Find the greatest common factor for each set of numbers.

	a		**b**
1. 7 and 3	_____	15 and 18	_____
2. 14 and 42	_____	27 and 18	_____
3. 36 and 24	_____	45 and 20	_____
4. 72 and 54	_____	42 and 49	_____
5. 86 and 94	_____	66 and 11	_____
6. 52 and 26	_____	12 and 40	_____
7. 9, 12, and 21	_____	16, 32, and 64	_____
8. 15, 25, and 40	_____	27, 36, and 72	_____

Lesson 1.8 Least Common Multiple

Find the least common multiple by listing multiples of each number until finding the first one that is shared.

8 — 8, 16, 24
12 — 12, 24 } The Least Common Multiple is 24.

Find the least common multiple for each set of numbers.

	a		**b**	
1.	51 and 18	_____	104 and 76	_____
2.	54 and 64	_____	20 and 26	_____
3.	78 and 110	_____	42 and 63	_____
4.	23 and 92	_____	75 and 15	_____
5.	28 and 32	_____	12 and 16	_____
6.	9, 45, and 81	_____	21, 45, and 6	_____
7.	17, 24, and 53	_____	86, 68, and 20	_____

Lesson 1.8 Least Common Multiple

Find the least common multiple for each set of numbers.

	a		**b**	
1.	10 and 13	_____	23 and 35	_____
2.	45 and 59	_____	41 and 55	_____
3.	68 and 71	_____	63 and 76	_____
4.	28 and 35	_____	40 and 50	_____
5.	33 and 44	_____	27 and 45	_____
6.	6, 76, and 18	_____	4, 24, and 21	_____
7.	5, 25, and 65	_____	7, 99, and 49	_____
8.	3, 27, and 45	_____	8, 72, and 216	_____

Lesson 1.9 Multiplying Decimals

The number of digits to the right of the decimal point in the product is the sum of the number of digits to the right of the decimal point of the factors.

$$
\begin{array}{r}
0.4 \\
\times\ 0.2 \\
\hline
0.08
\end{array}
\qquad
\begin{array}{r}
0.28 \\
\times\ 0.6 \\
\hline
0.168
\end{array}
\qquad
\begin{array}{r}
3.2432 \\
\times\ \ 0.13 \\
\hline
97296 \\
+\ 32432 \\
\hline
0.421616
\end{array}
$$

If needed, add zeros as place holders.

Multiply.

	a	b	c	d	e
1.	$\begin{array}{r}0.7\\ \times\ \ \ 8\\ \hline\end{array}$	$\begin{array}{r}0.08\\ \times\ \ 0.5\\ \hline\end{array}$	$\begin{array}{r}0.325\\ \times\ \ \ \ 0.3\\ \hline\end{array}$	$\begin{array}{r}1.68\\ \times\ \ \ \ 8\\ \hline\end{array}$	$\begin{array}{r}25\\ \times\ 0.7\\ \hline\end{array}$
2.	$\begin{array}{r}0.03\\ \times\ 3.06\\ \hline\end{array}$	$\begin{array}{r}0.162\\ \times\ \ \ \ 0.3\\ \hline\end{array}$	$\begin{array}{r}8.03\\ \times\ \ 3.5\\ \hline\end{array}$	$\begin{array}{r}0.297\\ \times\ \ \ \ 7.1\\ \hline\end{array}$	$\begin{array}{r}76.4\\ \times\ \ 3.6\\ \hline\end{array}$
3.	$\begin{array}{r}53.64\\ \times\ \ 0.37\\ \hline\end{array}$	$\begin{array}{r}328.1\\ \times\ \ 0.63\\ \hline\end{array}$	$\begin{array}{r}9.806\\ \times\ \ \ \ 31\\ \hline\end{array}$	$\begin{array}{r}600.3\\ \times\ 0.034\\ \hline\end{array}$	$\begin{array}{r}895\\ \times\ 0.63\\ \hline\end{array}$
4.	$\begin{array}{r}27.1\\ \times\ 3.54\\ \hline\end{array}$	$\begin{array}{r}3.263\\ \times\ \ \ \ 18\\ \hline\end{array}$	$\begin{array}{r}1.253\\ \times\ \ \ \ 12\\ \hline\end{array}$	$\begin{array}{r}58.9\\ \times\ 0.038\\ \hline\end{array}$	$\begin{array}{r}0.82\\ \times\ 0.82\\ \hline\end{array}$
5.	$\begin{array}{r}0.283\\ \times\ \ \ \ 0.6\\ \hline\end{array}$	$\begin{array}{r}0.178\\ \times\ \ \ \ 53\\ \hline\end{array}$	$\begin{array}{r}0.83\\ \times\ 0.23\\ \hline\end{array}$	$\begin{array}{r}3.6\\ \times\ 0.025\\ \hline\end{array}$	$\begin{array}{r}48.2\\ \times\ 0.26\\ \hline\end{array}$

Lesson 1.10 Dividing by Two Digits

Multiply the divisor and dividend by 10, by 100, or by 1,000 so the divisor is a whole number.

$$3.5\overline{)140.} = 3.5\overline{)140}$$
Multiply
by 10.

$$\begin{array}{r} 4 \\ 3.5\overline{)140} \\ -140 \\ \hline 0 \end{array}$$

$$0.42\overline{)16.80} = 42\overline{)1680}$$
Multiply
by 100.

$$\begin{array}{r} 40 \\ 42\overline{)1680} \\ -168 \\ \hline 0 \end{array}$$

$$0.27\overline{)8100.} = 27\overline{)8100}$$
Multiply
by 1,000.

$$\begin{array}{r} 300 \\ 27\overline{)8100} \\ -8100 \\ \hline 0 \end{array}$$

Divide.

	a	b	c	d
1.	$2.3\overline{)5.06}$	$3.4\overline{)289}$	$5.2\overline{)2.08}$	$7.2\overline{)10.8}$
2.	$0.45\overline{)18}$	$0.22\overline{)1.166}$	$0.63\overline{)25.2}$	$0.98\overline{)63.7}$
3.	$0.032\overline{)96}$	$0.015\overline{)0.45}$	$0.068\overline{)0.017}$	$0.012\overline{)0.0144}$
4.	$2.4\overline{)0.96}$	$0.62\overline{)24.8}$	$0.016\overline{)0.08}$	$0.85\overline{)5.1}$

Lesson 1.11 Problem Solving

SHOW YOUR WORK

Solve each problem.

1. A package weighs 2.6 pounds. How much do 8 of the same-sized packages weigh?

The packages weigh _____ pounds.

2. It takes Maxine 0.3 hours to make a potholder. How many potholders can she make in 4.5 hours?

She can make _____ potholders.

3. A box of grass seed weighs 0.62 pounds. How much does a box containing 0.75 times as much grass seed weigh?

The box weighs _____ pounds.

4. A collection of nickels is worth $18.60. How many nickels are in the collection?

There are _____ nickels in the collection.

5. Mrs. Anderson bought party favors for the 24 students in her class. Each favor costs $2.27. How much did all the party favors cost?

The favors cost _____.

6. Each prize for a carnival booth costs $0.32. How many prizes can you buy with $96?

You can buy _____ prizes.

7. Brittany has a pack of 24 pencils. Each pencil weighs 0.9 grams. How much does the pack of pencils weigh?

The pack of pencils weighs _____ grams.

1.

2.

3.

4.

5.

6.

7.

Lesson 1.11 Problem Solving

Solve each problem.

1. Workers are using a piece of iron that is 0.324 millimeters thick and a piece of copper that is 0.671 millimeters thick. How much thicker is the copper?

   The copper is _____ millimeters thicker.

2. Lenora bought a book for $12.36 and some school supplies for $7.29 and $5.47. How much did she spend?

   She spent _____.

3. Joe's bill at the grocery store came to $6.08. He paid with a ten-dollar bill and a dime. How much change did he get?

   He received _____ in change.

4. One bottle holds 67.34 ounces and another bottle holds 48.5 ounces. Combined, how much do they hold?

   The bottles hold _____ ounces combined.

5. A basic stereo system costs $189.67. An upgraded model costs $212.09. How much more does the upgraded model cost?

   The upgraded model costs _____ more.

6. Lin ran 0.683 kilometers on Wednesday and 0.75 kilometers on Thursday. How far did he run on the two days combined?

   He ran _____ kilometers over both days.

7. A certain cabinet door is actually made of three thin boards that are pressed together. The boards are 0.371 inches, 0.13 inches, and 0.204 inches thick. How thick is the cabinet door?

   The door is _____ inches thick.

1.

2.

3.

4.

5.

6.

7.

Check What You Learned

Understanding the Number System and Operations

Rewrite each expression using the Distributive Property.

	a	b

1. $3 \times (5 - 2) =$ _____ $(5 \times 2) + (8 \times 2) =$ _____

2. $7 \times (7 - 4) =$ _____ $(7 \times 6) - (7 \times 3) =$ _____

3. $3 \times (8 + 2) =$ _____ $5 \times (9 - 4) =$ _____

Find the Greatest Common Factor of each set of numbers.

	a	b	c

4. 40, 4 _____   30, 12 _____   4, 10 _____

5. 20, 24 _____   3, 10 _____   24, 2 _____

Find the Least Common Multiple of each set of numbers.

6. 30, 15 _____   15, 5 _____   20, 4 _____

7. 5, 12, 10 _____   3, 8 _____   40, 3, 24 _____

Check What You Learned

Understanding the Number System and Operations

Multiply or divide.

	a	**b**	**c**	**d**
8.	213 × 362	248 × 231	2851 × 261	3732 × 531

9. 76)6308   45)8329   26)45702   86)99588

	a	**b**	**c**	**d**
10.	365.3 × 5.2	0.76 × 0.53	$67.45 × 23	4.26 × 7.62

11. 0.6)78   0.09)738   0.07)50.4   18)$13.50

Solve each problem.

12. A bag of wood chips weighs 12.4 pounds. How much does a bag containing 0.42 times as many wood chips weigh?

The bag weighs _____ pounds.

13. One comic book costs $2.23. How many comic books can you buy for $71.36?

You can buy _____ comic books.

12.

13.

Check What You Know

Multiplying and Dividing Fractions

Multiply or divide. Write answers in simplest form.

	a	b	c
1.	$\frac{7}{8} \times \frac{3}{4}$	$9 \times \frac{3}{8}$	$\frac{5}{8} \times 5$
2.	$3\frac{1}{8} \times 4$	$8 \times 2\frac{3}{5}$	$4\frac{1}{2} \times 9$
3.	$5\frac{3}{4} \times 2\frac{1}{3}$	$2\frac{1}{4} \times 3\frac{1}{5}$	$3\frac{2}{3} \times 1\frac{1}{8}$
4.	$8 \div \frac{2}{3}$	$\frac{4}{5} \div 3$	$10 \div \frac{3}{8}$
5.	$\frac{4}{5} \div \frac{7}{8}$	$\frac{2}{3} \div \frac{5}{6}$	$\frac{3}{8} \div \frac{7}{8}$
6.	$2\frac{3}{4} \div 3\frac{1}{8}$	$7 \div 3\frac{1}{4}$	$7\frac{3}{8} \div 9$

Check What You Know

SHOW YOUR WORK

Multiplying and Dividing Fractions

Solve each problem. Write answers in simplest form.

7. John and George together raked $\frac{7}{8}$ of the yard. John raked $\frac{3}{4}$ of that amount. What part of the yard did John rake?

John raked _____ of the yard.

7.

8. Felipe has track practice for $\frac{5}{8}$ of an hour after school each day. How many hours does he have track practice in 5 days?

Felipe has track practice for _____ hours.

8.

9. Paul can walk $2\frac{1}{2}$ miles in 1 hour. How far can he walk in $1\frac{3}{4}$ hours?

Paul can walk _____ miles.

9.

10. Brad has a stack of 7 books on his desk. Each book is $1\frac{7}{8}$ inches thick. How tall is the stack?

The stack is _____ inches tall.

10.

11. A bag of candy weighs $3\frac{2}{3}$ ounces. How much would $4\frac{1}{2}$ bags of candy weigh?

The bags would weigh _____ ounces.

11.

12. It takes 8 hours to paint a room. How long will it take to paint $\frac{2}{3}$ of the room?

It will take _____ hours to paint $\frac{2}{3}$ of the room.

12.

13. Jim will divide $6\frac{3}{4}$ pounds of candy equally among 9 friends. How much candy will each friend get?

Each friend will get _____ of a pound.

13.

Lesson 2.1   Multiplying Fractions and Mixed Numbers

Multiply fractions.

$\frac{3}{8} \times \frac{2}{3} = \frac{3 \times 2}{8 \times 3}$ Multiply numerators together.
Multiply denominators together.

$= \frac{6}{24} = \frac{1}{4}$ Simplify.

Multiply mixed numbers.

$2\frac{3}{4} \times 3\frac{1}{3} = \frac{11}{4} \times \frac{10}{3}$ Rename each mixed number as an improper fraction.

$\frac{11}{4} \times \frac{10}{3} = \frac{110}{12} = \frac{55}{6}$ Multiply.

$= 9\frac{1}{6}$ Simplify.

Multiply. Write answers in simplest form.

	a	b	c	d
1.	$\frac{2}{5} \times \frac{2}{3} =$	$\frac{3}{4} \times \frac{5}{6} =$	$\frac{7}{8} \times \frac{5}{7} =$	$\frac{2}{5} \times \frac{3}{4} =$
2.	$\frac{7}{12} \times \frac{3}{4} =$	$\frac{2}{3} \times \frac{8}{9} =$	$\frac{4}{5} \times \frac{3}{8} =$	$\frac{3}{7} \times \frac{3}{5} =$
3.	$\frac{1}{6} \times \frac{2}{3} =$	$\frac{11}{12} \times \frac{2}{3} =$	$\frac{2}{5} \times \frac{2}{5} =$	$\frac{3}{4} \times \frac{3}{7} =$
4.	$1\frac{1}{3} \times 2\frac{1}{8} =$	$2\frac{1}{2} \times 1\frac{3}{4} =$	$2\frac{5}{8} \times 2\frac{3}{5} =$	$1\frac{1}{2} \times 2\frac{2}{3} =$
5.	$3\frac{1}{5} \times 5\frac{2}{3} =$	$4\frac{1}{2} \times 4\frac{1}{2} =$	$2\frac{1}{3} \times 3\frac{1}{4} =$	$2\frac{4}{5} \times 3\frac{1}{8} =$
6.	$2\frac{2}{3} \times 5\frac{1}{4} =$	$2\frac{1}{3} \times 2\frac{1}{3} =$	$3\frac{1}{4} \times 1\frac{1}{8} =$	$2\frac{7}{8} \times 1\frac{1}{3} =$

Lesson 2.2 Using Visual Models to Divide Fractions

Fraction bars can be used to help divide fractions.

| $\frac{1}{3}$ | | |

| $\frac{1}{6}$ | | | | | |

When dividing $\frac{1}{3}$ by $\frac{1}{6}$, you are finding out how many sixths are equal to $\frac{1}{3}$. When you line up the fraction bars and divide them into the appropriate pieces, you can see that $\frac{2}{6}$ is equal to $\frac{1}{3}$.

Therefore,

$$\frac{1}{3} \div \frac{1}{6} = 2$$

Use the fraction bars to solve the problems. Write answers in simplest form.

1. $\frac{1}{2} \div \frac{1}{4} = $ _____

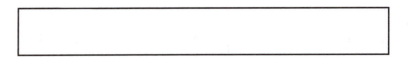

2. $\frac{2}{3} \div \frac{1}{6} = $ _____

3. $\frac{3}{5} \div \frac{1}{15} = $ _____

Lesson 2.2 Using Visual Models to Divide Fractions

Use the fraction bars to solve the problems. Write answers in simplest form.

1. $\frac{1}{8} \div \frac{1}{2} =$ _____

2. $\frac{1}{10} \div \frac{2}{5} =$ _____

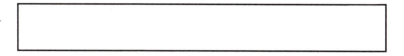

3. $\frac{1}{12} \div \frac{1}{4} =$ _____

4. $\frac{2}{9} \div \frac{1}{3} =$ _____

Lesson 2.3 Dividing Fractions

To divide, multiply by the reciprocal of the divisor.

$\frac{4}{5} \div \frac{8}{9} = \frac{4}{5} \times \frac{9}{8} = \frac{36}{40} = \frac{9}{10}$

Divide. Write answers in simplest form.

	a	b	c	d
1.	$\frac{1}{2} \div \frac{3}{5}$	$\frac{3}{8} \div \frac{2}{3}$	$\frac{5}{8} \div \frac{3}{4}$	$\frac{2}{5} \div \frac{3}{8}$
2.	$\frac{1}{2} \div \frac{7}{8}$	$\frac{4}{5} \div \frac{3}{4}$	$\frac{5}{6} \div \frac{3}{8}$	$\frac{2}{3} \div \frac{4}{5}$
3.	$\frac{7}{8} \div \frac{1}{3}$	$\frac{7}{9} \div \frac{2}{3}$	$\frac{1}{3} \div \frac{2}{3}$	$\frac{5}{6} \div \frac{1}{3}$
4.	$\frac{3}{5} \div \frac{2}{3}$	$\frac{4}{9} \div \frac{3}{7}$	$\frac{1}{2} \div \frac{5}{8}$	$\frac{2}{3} \div \frac{7}{9}$

Lesson 2.3 Dividing Fractions

Divide. Write answers in simplest form.

	a	b	c	d
1.	$\frac{3}{5} \div \frac{2}{7} =$	$\frac{3}{4} \div \frac{1}{2} =$	$\frac{5}{8} \div \frac{3}{5} =$	$\frac{5}{6} \div \frac{1}{10} =$
2.	$\frac{1}{5} \div \frac{1}{4} =$	$\frac{1}{2} \div \frac{2}{3} =$	$\frac{6}{7} \div \frac{1}{8} =$	$\frac{1}{4} \div \frac{1}{2} =$
3.	$\frac{7}{10} \div \frac{1}{4} =$	$\frac{1}{2} \div \frac{6}{11} =$	$\frac{3}{5} \div \frac{1}{3} =$	$\frac{1}{4} \div \frac{3}{8} =$
4.	$\frac{10}{12} \div \frac{2}{7} =$	$\frac{1}{15} \div \frac{4}{5} =$	$\frac{12}{15} \div \frac{1}{4} =$	$\frac{4}{5} \div \frac{9}{10} =$
5.	$\frac{9}{10} \div \frac{2}{6} =$	$\frac{7}{15} \div \frac{8}{10} =$	$\frac{2}{12} \div \frac{3}{4} =$	$\frac{7}{15} \div \frac{7}{9} =$

Lesson 2.3 Dividing Fractions

Divide. Write answers in simplest form.

	a	b	c	d
1.	$\frac{4}{9} \div \frac{1}{3} =$	$12 \div \frac{1}{5} =$	$2 \div \frac{2}{3} =$	$\frac{1}{5} \div \frac{1}{3} =$
2.	$\frac{1}{7} \div \frac{3}{5} =$	$\frac{2}{3} \div \frac{3}{4} =$	$5 \div \frac{2}{3} =$	$\frac{2}{3} \div \frac{1}{9} =$
3.	$\frac{7}{8} \div 4 =$	$\frac{2}{15} \div \frac{15}{17} =$	$\frac{3}{8} \div \frac{2}{3} =$	$\frac{3}{11} \div \frac{17}{23} =$
4.	$\frac{4}{11} \div \frac{2}{3} =$	$\frac{1}{11} \div \frac{5}{7} =$	$\frac{9}{20} \div \frac{9}{17} =$	$\frac{3}{7} \div \frac{9}{20} =$
5.	$\frac{2}{3} \div \frac{10}{11} =$	$\frac{1}{13} \div \frac{3}{13} =$	$\frac{6}{11} \div \frac{5}{7} =$	$\frac{1}{4} \div \frac{6}{17} =$

Lesson 2.4 Dividing Mixed Numbers

$3\frac{2}{5} \div 4$ Rename $3\frac{2}{5}$ as $\frac{17}{5}$.

$\frac{17}{5} \div \frac{4}{1}$ Rename 4 as $\frac{4}{1}$.

$\frac{9}{20} \times \frac{1}{4} = \frac{17}{20}$ Multiply by the reciprocal.

$4\frac{1}{3} \div 2\frac{3}{4}$

$\frac{13}{3} \div \frac{11}{4}$ Rename.

$\frac{13}{3} \times \frac{4}{11} = \frac{52}{33} = 1\frac{19}{33}$ Multiply by the reciprocal.

Divide. Write answers in simplest form.

	a	b	c	d
1.	$2\frac{1}{2} \div 3\frac{1}{3}$	$1\frac{1}{8} \div 2\frac{1}{4}$	$8 \div 3\frac{1}{2}$	$2\frac{1}{3} \div 5$
2.	$4\frac{1}{2} \div 1\frac{1}{6}$	$4\frac{5}{6} \div 2\frac{2}{5}$	$4\frac{1}{3} \div 6$	$1\frac{1}{2} \div 3\frac{1}{8}$
3.	$6 \div 2\frac{1}{2}$	$1\frac{1}{2} \div 3$	$5 \div 3\frac{3}{4}$	$2\frac{1}{8} \div 3$
4.	$3\frac{3}{5} \div 4$	$3\frac{1}{3} \div 2\frac{3}{8}$	$1 \div 4\frac{1}{3}$	$9 \div 1\frac{2}{3}$

Lesson 2.4 Dividing Mixed Numbers

Divide. Write answers in simplest form.

	a	b	c	d
1.	$1\frac{3}{4} \div \frac{2}{3} =$	$9 \div 1\frac{2}{3} =$	$\frac{4}{9} \div 1\frac{3}{5} =$	$4\frac{1}{4} \div 6 =$
2.	$1\frac{5}{6} \div \frac{1}{3} =$	$2\frac{2}{3} \div \frac{1}{4} =$	$\frac{4}{7} \div 1\frac{3}{4} =$	$2\frac{5}{6} \div 1\frac{2}{5} =$
3.	$3\frac{1}{4} \div 4 =$	$3\frac{1}{4} \div 4\frac{5}{8} =$	$3\frac{2}{7} \div 4\frac{1}{3} =$	$4\frac{4}{5} \div 4\frac{1}{2} =$
4.	$3\frac{1}{5} \div 4\frac{3}{7} =$	$2\frac{8}{9} \div 3\frac{4}{5} =$	$2\frac{1}{6} \div 4\frac{1}{9} =$	$3\frac{1}{2} \div 3\frac{1}{4} =$
5.	$5\frac{2}{5} \div 3\frac{1}{3} =$	$7 \div 2\frac{3}{8} =$	$4\frac{2}{7} \div 3\frac{1}{3} =$	$2\frac{2}{3} \div 3\frac{6}{11} =$

Lesson 2.5 Problem Solving

Solve each problem. Write answers in simplest form.

1. Sam and José mowed $\frac{2}{3}$ of the yard. José mowed $\frac{3}{4}$ of that amount. What part of the yard did José mow?

   José mowed _____ of the yard.

2. Maria practices the piano $\frac{5}{6}$ of an hour every day. How many hours does she practice in 4 days?

   Maria practices _____ hours.

3. It takes 6 hours to clean the Smith's house. How long does it take to clean $\frac{5}{8}$ of the house?

   It takes _____ hours.

4. A container holding $6\frac{2}{3}$ pints of juice will be divided equally among 5 people. How much juice will each person get?

   Each person will get _____ pints.

5. A 7-hour class will be divided into equal sessions of $1\frac{2}{5}$ hours. How many sessions will be needed?

   _____ sessions will be needed.

6. Jamie divided $6\frac{2}{5}$ ounces of candy into equal amounts. He put the candy into containers that hold $2\frac{2}{3}$ ounces each. How many containers will be filled?

   _____ containers will be filled.

7. Dawson baked one pie in $\frac{7}{12}$ of an hour. How long will it take Dawson to bake 9 pies?

   Dawson will bake 9 pies in _____ hours.

1.

2.

3.

4.

5.

6.

7.

Lesson 2.5 Problem Solving

SHOW YOUR WORK

Solve each problem. Write answers in simplest form.

1. How many pieces of string that are $\frac{2}{7}$ of an inch long can be cut from a piece of string that is $\frac{7}{8}$ of an inch long?

   _____ pieces of string can be cut.

2. Five pounds of walnuts will be divided equally into containers which will hold $\frac{5}{8}$ of a pound each. How many containers will be filled?

   _____ containers will be filled.

3. A ribbon is $\frac{7}{9}$ of a yard long. It will be divided equally among 3 people. What is the length of ribbon that each person will get?

   Each person will get _____ of a yard.

4. Raul can ride his bike $7\frac{1}{2}$ miles in one hour. How far can he ride in $2\frac{1}{3}$ hours?

   Raul can ride _____ miles.

5. If 8 boards are stacked on top of each other and each board is $2\frac{1}{4}$ inches thick, how high is the stack?

   The stack is _____ inches high.

6. A bag of potatoes weighs $2\frac{1}{2}$ pounds. How much would $3\frac{1}{3}$ bags weigh?

   The bags would weigh _____ pounds.

7. Jason put 6 pieces of chain together to make a fence. Each piece of chain was $3\frac{2}{5}$ feet long. How long was the chain?

   The chain was _____ feet long.

1.

2.

3.

4.

5.

6.

7.

Check What You Learned

Multiplying and Dividing Fractions

Multiply. Write answers in simplest form.

	a	b	c	d
1.	$\frac{2}{3} \times \frac{3}{4}$	$\frac{1}{2} \times \frac{3}{8}$	$\frac{7}{8} \times \frac{3}{5}$	$\frac{2}{7} \times \frac{5}{8}$
2.	$\frac{2}{3} \times 5$	$4 \times \frac{7}{8}$	$\frac{3}{5} \times 12$	$8 \times \frac{4}{7}$
3.	$3\frac{1}{8} \times 4$	$5 \times 7\frac{1}{2}$	$3\frac{2}{3} \times 6$	$10 \times 1\frac{2}{3}$
4.	$2\frac{1}{2} \times 3\frac{1}{3}$	$1\frac{1}{5} \times 3\frac{3}{4}$	$2\frac{1}{2} \times 2\frac{1}{2}$	$4\frac{1}{3} \times 2\frac{3}{5}$

Write the reciprocal.

5.	$\frac{3}{8}$ _____	5 _____	$\frac{12}{5}$ _____	$\frac{4}{7}$ _____

Divide. Write answers in simplest form.

6.	$5 \div \frac{2}{3}$	$\frac{4}{5} \div 5$	$7 \div \frac{3}{8}$	$\frac{7}{8} \div 2$
7.	$\frac{2}{3} \div \frac{4}{5}$	$\frac{7}{8} \div \frac{2}{3}$	$\frac{4}{7} \div \frac{3}{8}$	$\frac{5}{12} \div \frac{3}{4}$
8.	$3\frac{1}{8} \div 2\frac{1}{2}$	$4\frac{2}{3} \div 3\frac{1}{2}$	$2\frac{3}{4} \div 2\frac{3}{4}$	$1\frac{1}{2} \div 3\frac{1}{8}$

CHAPTER 2 POSTTEST

Check What You Learned

Multiplying and Dividing Fractions

Solve each problem. Write answers in simplest form.

9. Alice and Samantha watered $\frac{5}{6}$ of the yard together. Samantha watered $\frac{1}{3}$ of that amount. What part of the yard did Samantha water?

   Samantha watered _____ of the yard.

   9.

10. Ramona sets aside $\frac{3}{4}$ of an hour for homework after school each day. How many hours does she do homework in 5 days?

    Ramona does _____ hours of homework in 5 days.

    10.

11. Anita can skate $3\frac{1}{3}$ miles in 1 hour. How far can she skate in $2\frac{1}{2}$ hours?

    Anita can skate _____ miles.

    11.

12. A stack of 5 bricks is on the driveway. Each brick is $2\frac{1}{3}$ inches thick. How high is the stack of bricks?

    The stack of bricks is _____ inches high.

    12.

13. At the grocery, the bags of oranges weigh $4\frac{1}{3}$ pounds. How much would $2\frac{1}{2}$ bags of oranges weigh?

    The bags would weigh _____ pounds.

    13.

14. It takes a baseball team 2 hours to complete a game. How long will it take to complete $\frac{2}{3}$ of the game?

    It will take _____ hours.

    14.

15. A bag holding $7\frac{1}{5}$ pounds of mixed nuts will be divided equally among 9 people. How many pounds of nuts will each person get?

    Each person will get _____ of a pound of nuts.

    15.

Check What You Know

Ratios, Rates, and Percents

Solve each proportion.

	a	b	c
1.	$\frac{7}{5} = \frac{28}{\square}$ _____	$\frac{4}{6} = \frac{\square}{21}$ _____	$\frac{6}{\square} = \frac{15}{20}$ _____
2.	$\frac{\square}{9} = \frac{14}{18}$ _____	$\frac{15}{18} = \frac{10}{\square}$ _____	$\frac{\square}{30} = \frac{13}{10}$ _____
3.	$\frac{10}{8} = \frac{\square}{24}$ _____	$\frac{11}{12} = \frac{44}{\square}$ _____	$\frac{\square}{2} = \frac{9}{6}$ _____
4.	$\frac{12}{\square} = \frac{4}{5}$ _____	$\frac{10}{14} = \frac{\square}{35}$ _____	$\frac{10}{\square} = \frac{25}{15}$ _____

Write the equivalent decimal and fraction for each percent.

	Percent	a Decimal	b Fraction	Percent	c Decimal	d Fraction
5.	15%	_____	_____	22%	_____	_____
6.	120%	_____	_____	54%	_____	_____
7.	36%	_____	_____	205%	_____	_____

For each fraction or decimal, write the equivalent percent.

	a	b	c
8.	$\frac{3}{25} =$ _____	$0.01 =$ _____	$\frac{2}{5} =$ _____
9.	$4.06 =$ _____	$\frac{1}{8} =$ _____	$0.6 =$ _____

Complete each sentence.

	a	b
10.	90% of 120 is _____.	18 is 40% of _____.
11.	3.6 is 5% of _____.	27 is _____% of 108.
12.	$37\frac{1}{2}$% of 64 is _____.	35 is 25% of _____.
13.	39 is _____% of 52.	28 is _____% of 20.
14.	110% of 55 is _____.	82 is _____% of 40.

NAME _____

Check What You Know

Ratios, Rates, and Percents

Solve each problem.

15. Corn costs $2 for 6 ears. Carmen bought 24 ears of corn. How much did she spend?

Carmen spent _____.

15.

16. Tomatoes are 5 for $2. Keith spent $8 on tomatoes. How many tomatoes did he get?

Keith got _____ tomatoes.

16.

17. Peaches are 8 for $2. Jill bought 12 peaches. How much did she spend?

Jill spent _____.

17.

18. Corn costs $2 for 6 ears. Isabel spent $3 on corn. How many ears did she get?

Isabel got _____ ears.

18.

19. At East Side Middle School, $\frac{3}{4}$ of the students ride the bus to school. What percent of the students ride the bus?

_____ of the students ride the bus.

19.

20. Morgan got $\frac{17}{20}$ of the questions on a science test correct. What percent of the questions did she get correct?

Morgan got _____ of the questions correct.

20.

21. The band at East Side Middle School lost 20 percent of its 230 members from last year. How many band members left?

_____ band members left.

21.

22. A sweater is on sale for 40 percent off its original price of $29.95. What is the amount of savings?

The savings is _____.

22.

Lesson 3.1 Understanding Ratios

A **ratio** compares 2 numbers. When written out, several phrases can show how the ratio should be written.

4 to 2	4:2	$\frac{4}{2}$ or $\frac{2}{1}$
6 out of 8	6:8	$\frac{6}{8}$ or $\frac{3}{4}$

Express each ratio as a fraction in simplest form.

a

b

1. 15 feet out of 36 feet _____   5 pounds to 35 pounds _____

2. 48 rainy days out of 60 days _____   28 snow days out of 49 days _____

3. 10 pints to 20 pints _____   40 cups to 55 cups _____

4. 10 miles out of 12 miles _____   28 red bikes out of 40 bikes _____

5. 18 beetles out of 72 insects _____   63 gallons to 84 gallons _____

6. 49 dimes out of 77 coins _____   12 cakes out of 36 cakes _____

7. 15 students out of 30 students _____   3 floors out of 18 floors _____

8. 36 meters out of 100 meters _____   14 hats out of 20 accessories _____

9. 80 scores out of 90 scores _____   2 sports out of 19 sports _____

10. 42 cars out of 124 cars _____   7 messages out of 84 messages _____

Lesson 3.1 Understanding Ratios

Ratios can be written based on the number of objects in a set.

There are 2 bottles of soda and 5 bottles of water in the refrigerator. Write the ratio of sodas to waters.

$\dfrac{2}{5}$

Express each ratio as a fraction in simplest form.

a

b

1. There are 2 cubes and 15 spheres in a geometry box. Write the ratio of spheres to cubes.

   _____

   There are 5 cars and 4 vans in a parking lot. Write the ratio of vans to cars.

   _____

2. There are 5 horses and 15 elephants in a circus. Write the ratio of elephants to horses.

   _____

   There are 16 horses and 14 elephants in a circus. Write the ratio of horses to elephants.

   _____

3. There are 11 blue marbles and 7 red marbles in a box. Write the ratio of red marbles to blue marbles.

   _____

   There are 12 apples and 15 oranges in a fruit basket. Write the ratio of apples to oranges.

   _____

4. There are 5 blue marbles and 16 red marbles in a box. Write the ratio of blue marbles to red marbles.

   _____

   There are 12 dogs and 7 cats in a park. Write the ratio of cats to dogs.

   _____

5. There are 14 cars and 7 vans in a parking lot. Write the ratio of cars to vans.

   _____

   There are 7 blue marbles and 8 red marbles in a bag. Write the ratio of red marbles to blue marbles.

   _____

6. There are 6 pennies and 10 dimes in a jar. Write the ratio of pennies to dimes.

   _____

   There are 24 butterflies and 16 snails on the ground. Write the ratio of butterflies to snails.

   _____

Lesson 3.2 Solving Ratios

A proportion can be used in problem solving.

The ratio of apples to oranges is 4 to 5. There are 20 oranges in the basket. How many apples are there?

$\frac{4}{5} = \frac{n}{20}$ Set up a proportion, using n for the missing number.

$4 \times 20 = 5 \times n$ Cross-multiply.

$\frac{80}{5} = n$ Solve for n.

$16 = n$ There are 16 apples.

Solve.

	a	b	c
1.	$\frac{1}{3} = \frac{n}{24}$ _____	$\frac{4}{9} = \frac{n}{36}$ _____	$\frac{5}{45} = \frac{n}{9}$ _____
2.	$\frac{3}{5} = \frac{n}{15}$ _____	$\frac{10}{70} = \frac{n}{7}$ _____	$\frac{25}{40} = \frac{n}{16}$ _____
3.	$\frac{7}{12} = \frac{n}{36}$ _____	$\frac{13}{26} = \frac{n}{4}$ _____	$\frac{7}{1} = \frac{n}{3}$ _____
4.	$\frac{8}{5} = \frac{n}{40}$ _____	$\frac{2}{6} = \frac{n}{33}$ _____	$\frac{5}{13} = \frac{n}{39}$ _____
5.	$\frac{5}{6} = \frac{n}{18}$ _____	$\frac{9}{8} = \frac{n}{32}$ _____	$\frac{2}{3} = \frac{n}{15}$ _____

Lesson 3.2 Solving Ratios

The missing number can appear any place in a proportion.
Solve the same way.

$$\frac{2}{3} = \frac{6}{n}$$

$$3 \times 6 = 2 \times n$$

$$\frac{18}{2} = n$$

$$9 = n$$

$$\frac{3}{5} = \frac{n}{10}$$

$$3 \times 10 = 5 \times n$$

$$\frac{30}{5} = n$$

$$6 = n$$

$$\frac{3}{n} = \frac{6}{8}$$

$$3 \times 8 = 6 \times n$$

$$\frac{24}{6} = n$$

$$4 = n$$

$$\frac{n}{4} = \frac{3}{6}$$

$$4 \times 3 = 6 \times n$$

$$\frac{12}{6} = n$$

$$2 = n$$

Solve.

	a	**b**	**c**
1.	$\frac{n}{3} = \frac{3}{9}$ _____	$\frac{5}{3} = \frac{15}{n}$ _____	$\frac{2}{n} = \frac{1}{4}$ _____
2.	$\frac{15}{30} = \frac{2}{n}$ _____	$\frac{4}{6} = \frac{n}{24}$ _____	$\frac{n}{7} = \frac{15}{21}$ _____
3.	$\frac{6}{n} = \frac{15}{20}$ _____	$\frac{n}{12} = \frac{9}{18}$ _____	$\frac{9}{2} = \frac{27}{n}$ _____
4.	$\frac{7}{9} = \frac{n}{63}$ _____	$\frac{15}{n} = \frac{12}{4}$ _____	$\frac{40}{100} = \frac{n}{25}$ _____
5.	$\frac{35}{n} = \frac{4}{8}$ _____	$\frac{16}{4} = \frac{36}{n}$ _____	$\frac{n}{12} = \frac{25}{30}$ _____

Lesson 3.3 Solving Ratio Problems

Tables can be used to help find missing values in real-life ratio problems.

A car can drive 60 miles on two gallons of gas. Create a table to find out how many miles the car can travel on 10 gallons of gas.

Gas	2 gallons	4 gallons	6 gallons	8 gallons	10 gallons
Miles	60 miles	120 miles	180 miles	240 miles	300 miles

Complete the tables to solve the ratio problems. Circle your answer in the table.

1. You can buy 4 cans of green beans at the market for $2.25. How much will it cost to buy 12 cans of beans?

Cans	4 cans	8 cans	12 cans
Cost	$2.25		

2. An ice-cream factory makes 180 quarts of ice cream in 2 hours. How many quarts could be made in 12 hours?

Ice Cream	180 quarts					
Hours	2 hours	4 hours	6 hours	8 hours		

3. A jet travels 650 miles in 3 hours. At this rate, how far could the jet fly in 9 hours?

Distance	650 miles		
Hours	3 hours		

4. A bakery can make 640 bagels in 4 hours. How many can they bake in 16 hours?

Bagels	640 bagels			
Hours	4 hours			

Lesson 3.4 Understanding Unit Rates

A **rate** is a special ratio that compares quantities of two different types of items—for example, *340 miles per 10 gallons (340 mi./10 gal.)*. In a **unit rate**, the second quantity is always 1, such as in *34 miles per gallon (34 mi./1 gal.)*. This allows you to see how many of the first item corresponds to just one of the second item.

Suppose you want to divide students equally between buses for a field trip. To see how many students should go on each bus, find the unit rate.

If there are 160 students and 4 buses, how many students should go on each bus?

$\frac{160}{4} = \frac{s}{1}$ To find the number of students for one bus, divide by the number of buses total.

$\frac{160}{4} = \frac{40}{1}$ The unit rate is $\frac{40}{1}$, or 40 students per bus.

SHOW YOUR WORK

Solve each problem by finding the unit rate.

1. John can create 20 paintings in 4 weeks. How many paintings can he create each week?

   1. _____

2. Sasha can walk 6 miles in 3 hours. If she has to walk 1 mile, how long will it take her?

   2. _____

3. Todd keeps his 4-room house very clean. It takes him 1 hour and 36 minutes to clean his whole house. How long does it take him to clean one room?

   3. _____

4. Victoria can make 8 necklaces in 4 days. How long does it take her to make one necklace?

   4. _____

5. Byron has his own bakery. He bakes 84 cakes each week. How many cakes can he make in one day?

   5. _____

6. Charlie buys 3 computer tables for $390. How much did he pay for each table?

   6. _____

Lesson 3.5 Problem Solving

SHOW YOUR WORK

Solve the problems below using ratios and unit rates.

1. Gas mileage is the number of miles you can drive on a gallon of gasoline. A test of a new car results in 440 miles driven on 20 gallons of gas. How far could you drive on 60 gallons of gas? _____

   What is the car's gas mileage? _____

   1.

2. An ice-cream factory makes 100 quarts of ice cream in 5 hours. How many quarts could be made in 36 hours? _____

   What was that rate per day? _____

   2.

3. A jet travels 590 miles in 5 hours. At this rate, how far could the jet fly in 10 hours? _____

   What is the rate of speed of the jet? _____

   3.

4. You can buy 5 cans of green beans at the Village Market for $2.30, or you can buy 10 of them at Best Food for $5.10.

   Which place is the better buy? _____

   4.

5. You can buy 3 apples at the Quick Stop for $1.29. You can buy 5 apples at Shop and Save for $2.45.

   Which place is the better buy? _____

   5.

6. A ferris wheel can accommodate 55 people in 15 minutes.

   How many people could ride the ferris wheel in 2 hours? _____

   What is the rate per hour? _____

   6.

Lesson 3.5 Problem Solving

Solve the problems below using ratios and unit rates.

1. Keith makes 9 out of every 10 free throws. Josie makes 10 out of every 12 free throws. Who is better at making free throws?

   _____ is better at making free throws.

2. Carl reads 3 books every week. Jonna reads 6 books a month. Ray reads 85 books a year. Who reads the most books?

   _____ reads the most books.

3. Mary runs 4 laps in 8 minutes. Nicole runs 12 laps in 18 minutes. Who runs faster?

   _____ runs faster.

4. CD City sells 5 CDs for $49. Music Land sells 8 CDs for $59.50. Which store is the better place to buy CDs?

   _____ is the better place to buy CDs.

5. Two classes are ordering pizza for a pizza party. Mrs. Jimenez's class has 10 students and is planning to share 4 large pizzas. Mr. Nichols's class has 8 students and will share 3 large pizzas. If everyone in each class will receive the same amount of pizza, will students in Mrs. Jimenez's class or Mr. Nichols's class receive more pizza?

   Students in _____ class will receive more pizza.

6. Laura earns $7 per hour baby-sitting for her neighbor. How much will Laura make if she baby-sits for 4 hours?

   Laura will make _____.

1.
2.
3.
4.
5.
6.

Lesson 3.6 Understanding Percents

The symbol **%** (percent) means $\frac{1}{100}$ or 0.01 (one hundredth).

$7\% = 7 \times \frac{1}{100}$ $6\% = 6 \times 0.01$ $23\% = 23 \times \frac{1}{100}$ $47\% = 47 \times 0.01$

$\qquad = \frac{7}{1} \times \frac{1}{100}$ $= 0.06$ $= \frac{23}{100}$ $= 0.47$

$\qquad = \frac{7}{100}$

Write the fraction and decimal for each percent. Write fractions in simplest form.

	Percent	Fraction	Decimal
1.	2%	_____	_____
2.	8%	_____	_____
3.	27%	_____	_____
4.	13%	_____	_____
5.	68%	_____	_____
6.	72%	_____	_____
7.	56%	_____	_____
8.	11%	_____	_____
9.	3%	_____	_____
10.	22%	_____	_____
11.	17%	_____	_____
12.	83%	_____	_____
13.	97%	_____	_____
14.	43%	_____	_____

Lesson 3.6 Understanding Percents

Write the fraction and decimal for each percent. Write fractions in simplest form.

	Percent	Fraction	Decimal
1.	7%	_____	_____
2.	13%	_____	_____
3.	48%	_____	_____
4.	71%	_____	_____
5.	27%	_____	_____
6.	2%	_____	_____
7.	15%	_____	_____
8.	39%	_____	_____
9.	10%	_____	_____
10.	62%	_____	_____
11.	75%	_____	_____
12.	97%	_____	_____
13.	53%	_____	_____
14.	82%	_____	_____

Lesson 3.7 Finding Percents Using Fractions

$35\% \text{ of } 60 = 35\% \times 60$

$\quad = \frac{35}{100} \times 60$

$\quad = \frac{7}{20} \times \frac{60}{1} = \frac{420}{20} = \frac{42}{2}$

$\quad = 21$

$40\% \text{ of } 32 =$

$40\% \times 32 = \frac{40}{100} \times 32$

$\quad = \frac{2}{5} \times \frac{32}{1} = \frac{64}{5}$

$\quad = 12\frac{4}{5}$

Complete the following. Write each answer in simplest form.

	a	b
1.	8% of 65 = _____	95% of 80 = _____
2.	30% of 32 = _____	25% of 28 = _____
3.	150% of 12 = _____	25% of 30 = _____
4.	28% of 7 = _____	10% of 38 = _____
5.	40% of 20 = _____	15% of 45 = _____
6.	80% of 80 = _____	20% of 75 = _____
7.	45% of 70 = _____	18% of 45 = _____
8.	4% of 92 = _____	16% of 90 = _____
9.	90% of 60 = _____	25% of 86 = _____
10.	12% of 40 = _____	9% of 60 = _____
11.	60% of 60 = _____	95% of 20 = _____
12.	21% of 50 = _____	3% of 25 = _____

Lesson 3.8 Finding Percents Using Decimals

26% of 73.2 $26\% = 26 \times 0.01 = 0.26$

$$
\begin{array}{r}
7\,3.2 \\
\times\quad 0.2\,6 \\
\hline
4\,3\,9\,2 \\
+\ 1\,4\,6\,4\quad \\
\hline
1\,9.0\,3\,2
\end{array}
$$

26% of 73.2 = 19.032

Complete the following.

	a	**b**
1.	32% of 64 = _____	26% of 40 = _____
2.	2.5% of 89 = _____	1.2% of 385 = _____
3.	58% of 12 = _____	250% of 8 = _____
4.	73% of 8.4 = _____	49% of 86 = _____
5.	0.8% of 256 = _____	11% of 29 = _____
6.	120% of 35 = _____	7.5% of 60 = _____
7.	84% of 7 = _____	40% of 95 = _____
8.	20% of 45 = _____	22% of 142 = _____
9.	9.2% of 63 = _____	80% of 80 = _____
10.	7% of 112 = _____	62% of 45 = _____
11.	16% of 16 = _____	12% of 200 = _____
12.	1.8% of 240 = _____	18% of 15 = _____

Lesson 3.9 Finding Percents

Use these methods to find the percent one number is of another number:

50 is what percent of 80?

$$50 = n\% \times 80$$

$$50 = \frac{n}{100} \times 80 \qquad 50 = \frac{80n}{100}$$

$$5000 = 80n$$

$$5000 \div 80 = 80n \div 80$$

$$62.5 = n$$

50 is 62.5% of 80.

$\frac{1}{4}$ is what percent of $\frac{5}{8}$?

$$\frac{1}{4} = n\% \times \frac{5}{8}$$

$$\frac{1}{4} = \frac{n}{100} \times \frac{5}{8} \qquad \frac{1}{4} = \frac{5n}{800}$$

$$800 = 20n$$

$$800 \div 20 = 20n \div 20$$

$$40 = n$$

$\frac{1}{4}$ is 40% of $\frac{5}{8}$.

Complete the following.

	a	b
1.	12 is _____ % of 20.	0.9 is _____ % of 4.5.
2.	15 is _____ % of 100.	16 is _____ % of 25.
3.	0.9 is _____ % of 6.	$\frac{1}{3}$ is _____ % of $\frac{5}{6}$.
4.	1.8 is _____ % of 18.	45 is _____ % of 50.
5.	48 is _____ % of 64.	16 is _____ % of 40.
6.	19 is _____ % of 95.	39 is _____ % of 26.
7.	1.8 is _____ % of 6.	5.6 is _____ % of 2.8.
8.	12 is _____ % of 32.	64 is _____ % of 51.2.
9.	$\frac{3}{8}$ is _____ % of $\frac{3}{4}$.	1.4 is _____ % of 5.6.
10.	0.6 is _____ % of 0.5.	$\frac{7}{10}$ is _____ % of $\frac{7}{8}$.

Lesson 3.10 Problem Solving

SHOW YOUR WORK

Solve each problem.

1. The sales tax on the purchase of a refrigerator that costs $695 is 7 percent. What is the amount of sales tax?

   The sales tax is _____.

2. A stove that costs $695 will be on sale next week for 28 percent off its regular price. What is the amount of savings?

   The savings will be _____.

3. In math class, 60 percent of the students are males. There are 30 students in the class. How many students are males?

   There are _____ males.

4. East Side Middle School has 1,500 students. Thirty-two percent of them are in sixth grade. How many sixth-grade students are there?

   There are _____ sixth-grade students.

5. Lauren is saving for gymnastics camp. Camp costs $225 to attend. She has 40 percent of the money saved. How much money has she saved?

   Lauren has saved _____.

6. Of the 1,500 students attending East Side Middle School, twenty-five percent are running for student council. How many students are running for student council?

   _____ students are running for student council.

1.

2.

3.

4.

5.

6.

Lesson 3.10 Problem Solving

SHOW YOUR WORK

Solve each problem.

1. The Jacksons' dinner cost $125. They left $21.25 for a tip. What percent did they tip?

   The Jacksons tipped _____.

2. A sweater was originally $55. It is now marked down to 65% of its original price. How much is the sweater now?

   The sweater now costs _____.

3. Ms. Martino's new home cost $260,000. She paid $39,000 in a down payment. What percent of the home cost did she pay in the down payment?

   Ms. Martino paid _____ of the total price.

4. Workers have painted 920 square feet of an office. They have completed 80% of their job. How many square feet do they need to paint in all?

   They need to paint _____ square feet.

5. The Franklins are taking a cross-country trip. They will drive 3,150 miles in all. On the first day, they drove 567 miles. What percent of their trip did they drive?

   The Franklins drove _____ of their trip.

6. Jen is reading a 276-page book. She is 25% finished. How many pages has she read?

   Jen has read _____ pages.

7. Pete's dog weighed 30 pounds. It then lost 16% of its weight. How much did Pete's dog lose?

   The dog lost _____ pounds.

8. Karla has read 85% of her book, which amounts to 238 pages. How long is the book?

   The book is _____ pages long.

1.

2.

3.

4.

5.

6.

7.

8.

Check What You Learned

Ratios, Rates, and Percents

Solve each proportion.

	a	b	c
1.	$\frac{\square}{12} = \frac{5}{4}$ _____	$\frac{18}{16} = \frac{\square}{24}$ _____	$\frac{2}{\square} = \frac{10}{15}$ _____
2.	$\frac{15}{21} = \frac{\square}{7}$ _____	$\frac{\square}{8} = \frac{18}{24}$ _____	$\frac{10}{14} = \frac{15}{\square}$ _____
3.	$\frac{5}{\square} = \frac{20}{24}$ _____	$\frac{4}{7} = \frac{\square}{28}$ _____	$\frac{8}{6} = \frac{20}{\square}$ _____
4.	$\frac{\square}{10} = \frac{21}{15}$ _____	$\frac{15}{\square} = \frac{20}{12}$ _____	$\frac{3}{12} = \frac{\square}{16}$ _____

Write the equivalent decimal and fraction for each percent.

		a	b		c	d
	Percent	Decimal	Fraction	Percent	Decimal	Fraction
5.	24%	_____	_____	110%	_____	_____
6.	37%	_____	_____	55%	_____	_____
7.	6%	_____	_____	235%	_____	_____

For each fraction or decimal, write the equivalent percent.

	a	b	c
8.	$\frac{4}{25} =$ _____	$0.05 =$ _____	$\frac{3}{5} =$ _____
9.	$0.8 =$ _____	$\frac{7}{8} =$ _____	$1.3 =$ _____

Complete each sentence.

	a	b
10.	24 is 30% of _____.	42 is _____% of 50.
11.	20% of 75 is _____.	112 is 70% of _____.
12.	6.2 is _____% of 124.	32% of 85 is _____.
13.	9 is 12.5% of _____.	7 is _____% of 56.
14.	125% of 48 is _____.	5.5 is 125% of _____.

Check What You Learned

SHOW YOUR WORK

Ratios, Rates, and Percents

Solve each problem.

15. Jeans are $20 for 2 pairs. Kerry spent $40 on jeans. How many pairs did she buy?

Kerry bought _____ pairs of jeans.

15.

16. Skirts are 4 for $30. Marta and her sisters bought 6 skirts. How much did they pay?

They paid _____.

16.

17. Sweaters are 3 for $50. Leslie and her mother spent $100 on sweaters. How many did they buy?

They bought _____ sweaters.

17.

18. T-shirts are 3 for $18. Tia bought 4 T-shirts. How much did she spend?

Tia spent _____.

18.

19. In Keon's homeroom class, $\frac{3}{5}$ of the students participate in sports. What percent of students participate in sports?

_____ participate in sports.

19.

20. Fifty-five percent of the students at West Side Middle School walk to school. What fraction of the students walk to school?

_____ of the students walk to school.

20.

21. A new car that costs $17,500 loses 25% of its value in the first year. How much is the loss of value?

The loss of value is _____.

21.

22. The 140-member chorus at West Side Middle School wants to add 30 percent more members next year. How many members do they want to add?

They want to add _____ members.

22.

Check What You Know

Integer Concepts

Name the opposite of each number.

a
b

1. The opposite of 8 is _____.   The opposite of −1 is _____.

2. The opposite of 5 is _____.   The opposite of 35 is _____.

3. The opposite of −21 is _____.   The opposite of −16 is _____.

Find the absolute value of each integer.

	a	**b**	**c**
4.	$|-3|$ = _____	$|10|$ = _____	$|5|$ = _____
5.	$|-9|$ = _____	$|23|$ = _____	$|-7|$ = _____
6.	$|-13|$ = _____	$|5|$ = _____	$|-1|$ = _____

Compare the integers using <, >, or =.

	a	**b**	**c**
7.	82 ☐ 91	31 ☐ −27	−44 ☐ −84
8.	23 ☐ 74	−10 ☐ 70	51 ☐ 24
9.	74 ☐ −42	99 ☐ 66	−23 ☐ −21

Order from least to greatest.

a
b

10. −89, 42, −26, 8 _____   −84, 91, −57, −90 _____

11. 20, −81, −5, 87 _____   73, 53, 89, 55 _____

12. −91, −46, 52, 12 _____   22, 41, −23, −38 _____

Check What You Know

Integer Concepts

Use the coordinate grid to answer the questions.

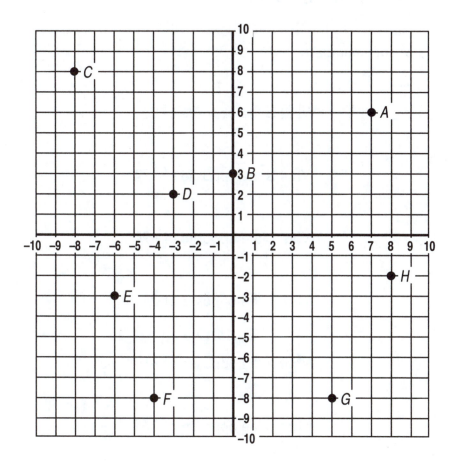

Write the ordered pair for each coordinate.

13. A _____

14. C _____

15. E _____

16. G _____

Name the point located at each ordered pair.

17. (8, −2) _____

18. (−3, 2) _____

19. (−4, −8) _____

20. (0, 3) _____

Mark the following points on the coordinate grid.

21. I at (4, −3)

22. J at (−8, −5)

23. K at (−5, −5)

24. L at (6, 2)

Spectrum Math
Grade 6

Lesson 4.1 Integers as Opposite Numbers

Every positive number has an opposite, negative number. A negative number is less than 0.

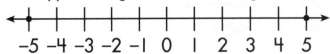

Draw a number line to show the opposite of each number.

a   **b**

1. What is the opposite of 8?   What is the opposite of 25?

2. What is the opposite of –10?   What is the opposite of –7?

3. What is the opposite of 12?   What is the opposite of –9?

4. What is the opposite of –6?   What is the opposite of 2?

5. What is the opposite of 11?   What is the opposite of –14?

6. What is the opposite of –20?   What is the opposite of 16?

Name the opposite of each number.

7. The opposite of 10 is _____.   The opposite of 1 is _____.

8. The opposite of –3 is _____.   The opposite of 7 is _____.

9. The opposite of –4 is _____.   The opposite of –8 is _____.

10. The opposite of 13 is _____.   The opposite of –15 is _____.

11. The opposite of –32 is _____.   The opposite of 27 is _____.

12. The opposite of 17 is _____.   The opposite of –20 is _____.

Lesson 4.2   Integer Values in Real Life

Integers can be used to describe real-life situations.

A driver is going 15 miles per hour below the speed limit. The integer −15 can describe this situation. The negative sign shows that the speed is less than the speed limit.

Use integers to represent each real-life situation.

	a	**b**
1.	45 feet below sea level _____	a gain of 8 yards on a play _____
2.	$528 deposit into a checking account _____	62° above zero _____
3.	stock market increases of 345 points _____	an 8-pound weight loss _____
4.	7,500 feet above sea level _____	withdrawal of $80 from an ATM _____
5.	a 10-pound weight gain _____	stock market decrease of 250 points _____
6.	3 units to the right on a number line _____	8 units to the left on a number line _____
7.	10 units to the left on a number line _____	7 units to the right on a number line _____
8.	$60 deposit into a savings account _____	withdrawal of $95 from an ATM _____
9.	stock market decrease of 97 points _____	34° below zero _____
10.	100 feet below sea level _____	a gain of 15 yards on a play _____
11.	a 25-pound weight loss _____	stock market increase of 390 points _____
12.	95° above zero _____	6,000 feet above sea level _____

Lesson 4.3 Absolute Value

The **absolute value** of a number is its distance from zero.

Absolute value is represented by vertical lines on either side of an integer.

What is the absolute value of 8? $|8| = 8$

What is the absolute value of –8? $|-8| = 8$

Find the absolute value of each integer.

	a	b	c
1.	$\lvert 4 \rvert = $ _____	$\lvert -13 \rvert = $ _____	$-\lvert 10 \rvert = $ _____
2.	$-\lvert -7 \rvert = $ _____	$\lvert 11 \rvert = $ _____	$\lvert -2 \rvert = $ _____
3.	$-\lvert 12 \rvert = $ _____	$-\lvert 5 \rvert = $ _____	$\lvert 1 \rvert = $ _____
4.	$\lvert -14 \rvert = $ _____	$-\lvert 8 \rvert = $ _____	$-\lvert -13 \rvert = $ _____
5.	$\lvert 3 \rvert = $ _____	$\lvert -7 \rvert = $ _____	$-\lvert 4 \rvert = $ _____
6.	$-\lvert -15 \rvert = $ _____	$\lvert 9 \rvert = $ _____	$\lvert -12 \rvert = $ _____
7.	$\lvert 16 \rvert = $ _____	$\lvert -6 \rvert = $ _____	$-\lvert 20 \rvert = $ _____
8.	$-\lvert 40 \rvert = $ _____	$-\lvert -24 \rvert = $ _____	$\lvert 17 \rvert = $ _____
9.	$\lvert 33 \rvert = $ _____	$-\lvert -41 \rvert = $ _____	$\lvert -19 \rvert = $ _____
10.	$\lvert 26 \rvert = $ _____	$\lvert -18 \rvert = $ _____	$-\lvert 35 \rvert = $ _____
11.	$-\lvert 53 \rvert = $ _____	$\lvert -21 \rvert = $ _____	$\lvert 30 \rvert = $ _____
12.	$\lvert 25 \rvert = $ _____	$-\lvert -21 \rvert = $ _____	$\lvert -47 \rvert = $ _____

Lesson 4.3 Absolute Value

Find the absolute value of each integer.

	a	b	c
1.	$|64| =$ _____	$|-81| =$ _____	$-|32| =$ _____
2.	$-|-8| =$ _____	$|19| =$ _____	$|-53| =$ _____
3.	$-|76| =$ _____	$-|3| =$ _____	$|11| =$ _____
4.	$|-62| =$ _____	$-|95| =$ _____	$-|-42| =$ _____
5.	$|2| =$ _____	$|-36| =$ _____	$-|9| =$ _____
6.	$-|-13| =$ _____	$|48| =$ _____	$|-27| =$ _____
7.	$|35| =$ _____	$|-29| =$ _____	$-|23| =$ _____
8.	$-|51| =$ _____	$|-57| =$ _____	$|80| =$ _____
9.	$|73| =$ _____	$-|-55| =$ _____	$|-46| =$ _____
10.	$|65| =$ _____	$|-37| =$ _____	$-|59| =$ _____
11.	$|-67| =$ _____	$|-70| =$ _____	$|50| =$ _____
12.	$|34| =$ _____	$-|-63| =$ _____	$|-71| =$ _____
13.	$|58| =$ _____	$|-93| =$ _____	$|-21| =$ _____
14.	$-|6| =$ _____	$-|-17| =$ _____	$-|88| =$ _____
15.	$|10| =$ _____	$|-49| =$ _____	$-|5| =$ _____
16.	$-|-22| =$ _____	$-|79| =$ _____	$|31| =$ _____

Lesson 4.4   Comparing and Ordering Integers

Integers are the set of whole numbers and their opposites.

Positive integers are greater than zero. **Negative integers** are less than zero. Zero is neither positive nor negative. A negative integer is less than a positive integer. On a number line, an integer and its opposite are the same distance from zero. The smaller of two integers is always the one to the left on a number line.

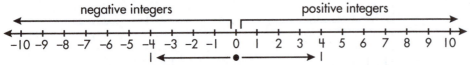

The opposite of 4 is −4. They are both 4 spaces from 0.

$$-7 < -2$$
−7 is to the left of −2.

$$-4 > -9$$
−4 is to the right of −9.

Use integers to name each point on the number line.

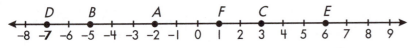

a	b	c
1. A _____	D _____	F _____
2. E _____	C _____	B _____

Use > or < to compare each pair of numbers.

3. 2 ☐ 7   −1 ☐ −4   5 ☐ 0

4. −4 ☐ 1   0 ☐ −8   −8 ☐ −10

5. 7 ☐ −7   −2 ☐ 0   4 ☐ 6

6. 1 ☐ −1   6 ☐ 3   −6 ☐ −3

7. 4 ☐ −2   −6 ☐ −4   3 ☐ −3

Order from least to greatest.

a	b
8. −3, −5, 0 _____	8, −8, 2 _____
9. 0, 5, −3, −7 _____	4, −1, 2, −2 _____
10. −6, 5, −2, −3, 2 _____	5, −8, −2, −3, 0 _____

Lesson 4.4 Comparing and Ordering Integers

Compare the integers using <, >, or =.

	a	**b**	**c**
1.	66 ☐ 3	43 ☐ 83	−24 ☐ 82
2.	99 ☐ −84	−33 ☐ −90	−37 ☐ −37
3.	28 ☐ 7	−24 ☐ 61	−36 ☐ −88
4.	−27 ☐ −52	−49 ☐ −69	42 ☐ 98
5.	88 ☐ −99	47 ☐ −44	−8 ☐ −45
6.	46 ☐ −26	13 ☐ −1	39 ☐ 51
7.	8 ☐ −18	61 ☐ −70	−4 ☐ −1
8.	−12 ☐ −14	−1 ☐ 0	57 ☐ −73

Order from least to greatest.

	a	**b**
9.	16, −37, 51, 61 _____	−86, 21, 90, −49 _____
10.	−84, −67, 10, −65 _____	−62, 11, −97, −78 _____
11.	−35, 81, −37, 48 _____	−68, −9, 95, 19 _____
12.	−37, 51, 61, 9 _____	21, 90, −49, 15 _____
13.	14, −4, 9, −11 _____	74, −23, 27, −75 _____
14.	−80, −79, 2, 81 _____	47, 93, −39, −47 _____

Lesson 4.4 Comparing and Ordering Integers

Compare the integers using <, >, or =.

a	b	c
1. 92 ☐ 35	−56 ☐ −57	−77 ☐ 37
2. 78 ☐ −96	−99 ☐ −94	34 ☐ −60
3. −1 ☐ −37	6 ☐ −78	34 ☐ −43
4. 4 ☐ −4	−66 ☐ −13	−66 ☐ −45
5. −10 ☐ 51	76 ☐ 13	−69 ☐ −79
6. 18 ☐ 80	−12 ☐ −81	−61 ☐ 57
7. 33 ☐ −64	17 ☐ 13	−21 ☐ 19
8. 18 ☐ 80	−12 ☐ −81	−61 ☐ 57

Order from least to greatest.

a	b
9. −67, 10, −65, 20 _____	11, −97, −78, −57 _____
10. 81, −37, 48, −39 _____	−9, 95, 19, −96 _____
11. 51, 61, 9, 47 _____	90, −49, 15, 22 _____
12. 10, −65, 20, 55 _____	−97, −78, −57, −68 _____
13. −16, −34, 14, 0 _____	72, −12, −7, 67 _____
14. 46, 52, −2, −46 _____	−3, −92, −51, −28 _____

Lesson 4.5 Using Integers in the Coordinate Plane

Positive and negative coordinates can be graphed using the coordinate plane system.

The first number in an ordered pair represents its point on the x-axis. The second number represents the point on the y-axis.

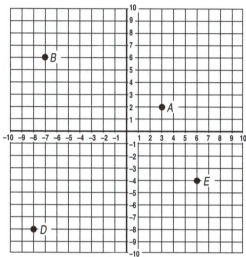

Point A: (3, 2)

Point B: (−7, 6)

Point C: (6, −4)

Point D: (−8, −8)

Use the coordinate grid to answer the questions.

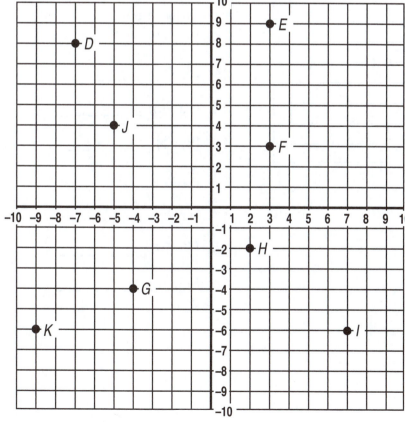

Write the ordered pair for each coordinate.

1. D _____

2. E _____

3. G _____

4. H _____

5. K _____

Name the point located at each ordered pair.

6. (−5, 4) _____

7. (7, −6) _____

8. (−9, −6) _____

9. (3, 3) _____

10. (−7, 8) _____

Lesson 4.5 Using Integers in the Coordinate Plane

Use the coordinate grid to answer the questions.

Write the ordered pair for each coordinate.

1. R _____

2. T _____

3. U _____

4. W _____

5. V _____

6. Q _____

7. S _____

8. X _____

Name the point located at each ordered pair.

9. (−2, 7) _____

10. (5, 7) _____

11. (−3, −3) _____

12. (4, −5) _____

13. (0, 4) _____

14. (7, 0) _____

15. (−8, 3) _____

16. (−6, −6) _____

Lesson 4.6 Problem Solving in the Coordinate Plane

Use the coordinate grid to answer the questions.

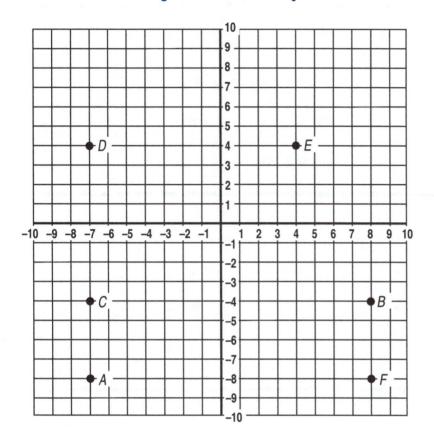

A – stream   D – school

B – home   E – park

C – bookstore   F – fire station

How far is it from the fire station to the bookstore?

Begin at the fire station.

First move __15__ units left. Then, move __4__ units up.

__15__ + __4__ = __19__ units

It takes __19__ units to get from the fire station to the bookstore.

1. How far is it from school to the park? _____ units

2. How far is it from the stream to the fire station? _____ units

3. How far is it from the bookstore to home? _____ units

4. How far is it from the stream to the school? _____ units

5. How far is from the fire station to home? _____ units

Check What You Learned

Integer Concepts

Name the opposite of each number.

a	b
1. The opposite of –9 is _____.	The opposite of 17 is _____.
2. The opposite of 22 is _____.	The opposite of –41 is _____.
3. The opposite of –5 is _____.	The opposite of 76 is _____.

Find the absolute value of each integer.

a	b	c
4. |3| = _____	–|10| = _____	|–45| = _____
5. –|–29| = _____	|12| = _____	|–8| = _____
6. |–26| = _____	|2| = _____	–|–18| = _____

Compare the integers using <, >, or =.

a	b	c
7. 92 ☐ 79	50 ☐ –76	–74 ☐ –35
8. –77 ☐ 15	–11 ☐ –49	–14 ☐ –73
9. –18 ☐ –76	44 ☐ 72	–45 ☐ –12

Order from least to greatest.

a	b
10. –70, 60, –28, 86 _____	–17, 45, –54, –38 _____
11. –97, –71, 36, –63 _____	–36, 60, 26, 63 _____
12. 38, 56, 89, 48 _____	49, 97, –47, 78 _____

Check What You Learned

Integer Concepts

Use the coordinate grid to answer the questions.

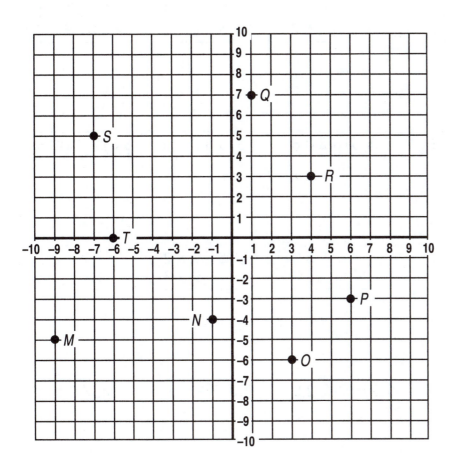

Write the ordered pair for each coordinate.

13. M _____

14. O _____

15. Q _____

16. S _____

Name the point located at each ordered pair.

17. (6, –3) _____

18. (–6, 0) _____

19. (–1, –4) _____

20. (4, 3) _____

CHAPTER 4 POSTTEST

Mark the following points on the coordinate grid.

21. U at (–3, 4)

22. V at (–5, –8)

23. W at (5, –5)

24. X at (2, 6)

25. How many units is it from Point P to Point M? _____ units

26. How many units is it from Point T to Point Q? _____ units

Mid-Test Chapters 1–4

Multiply or divide. Write fractions in simplest form.

	a	b	c	d	e
1.	329×17	1843×51	432×57	2945×612	6281×408
2.	$58\overline{)704}$	$8\overline{)62472}$	$45\overline{)6208}$	$15\overline{)38725}$	$68\overline{)29104}$
3.	6.4×8.7	0.786×0.41	$\$67.52 \times 20$	$\$16.52 \times 6.93$	27.63×6
4.	$0.5\overline{)37.5}$	$0.07\overline{)46.55}$	$6.3\overline{)476.28}$	$0.3\overline{)742.8}$	$1.8\overline{)705.6}$
5.	$\frac{2}{3} \times \frac{3}{4} =$	$\frac{5}{6} \times \frac{7}{8} =$	$6 \times \frac{5}{8} =$	$2 \times 4\frac{2}{3} =$	$3\frac{1}{3} \times 4\frac{1}{5} =$
6.	$5 \div \frac{1}{6} =$	$\frac{3}{5} \div 4 =$	$\frac{7}{8} \div \frac{2}{3} =$	$4\frac{1}{3} \div 5 =$	$3\frac{1}{8} \div 1\frac{2}{3} =$

CHAPTERS 1–4 MID-TEST

Mid-Test Chapters 1–4

Find the unknown value in each ratio.

	a	b	c
7.	$\frac{9}{2} = \frac{18}{\square}$ _____	$\frac{5}{11} = \frac{\square}{77}$ _____	$\frac{\square}{36} = \frac{5}{12}$ _____
8.	$\frac{12}{7} = \frac{48}{\square}$ _____	$\frac{42}{\square} = \frac{7}{3}$ _____	$\frac{4}{9} = \frac{\square}{54}$ _____
9.	$\frac{9}{\square} = \frac{54}{66}$ _____	$\frac{\square}{7} = \frac{14}{49}$ _____	$\frac{5}{4} = \frac{10}{\square}$ _____

SHOW YOUR WORK

Find the unit rate for each problem.

10. The Wilson Student Government sold $126 worth of tickets for a talent show in 3 hours. How many tickets did they sell in one hour?

They sold _____ tickets in one hour.

11. One thousand sixty-five people visited the carnival in 5 hours. How many people visited in one hour?

_____ people visited in one hour.

12. You can buy 6 apples at Shop and Save for $0.96. You can buy 4 of the same apples at Value Food for $1.20. Which store has the better buy?

_____ has the better buy.

10.

11.

12.

Convert to percents.

	a	b	c
13.	$\frac{3}{20} =$ _____	$\frac{4}{5} =$ _____	$\frac{14}{50} =$ _____

Convert to decimals.

14.	30% = _____	$72\frac{1}{4}\% =$ _____	346% = _____

Convert to fractions.

15.	75% = _____	20% = _____	140% = _____

CHAPTERS 1–4 MID-TEST

Mid-Test Chapters 1–4

Complete each statement.

	a	b	c

16. _____ is 9% of 30.   _____ is 8% of 15.   _____ is 22% of 90.

17. 36.9 is 45% of _____.   0.36 is 12% of _____.   120 is 150% of _____.

18. 13 is _____% of 52.   5 is _____% of 125.   38 is _____% of 40.

Find the absolute value of each integer.

19. $|7| =$ _____ $|71| =$ _____ $-|-68| =$ _____

20. $|-100| =$ _____ $-|25| =$ _____ $|95| =$ _____

21. $-|37| =$ _____ $|-68| =$ _____ $-|-25| =$ _____

Compare the integers using $<$, $>$, or $=$.

22. $-32 \ \Box \ -35$ $-68 \ \Box \ -41$ $40 \ \Box \ 27$

23. $96 \ \Box \ 17$ $20 \ \Box \ 36$ $20 \ \Box \ 48$

24. $72 \ \Box \ -15$ $-29 \ \Box \ 62$ $14 \ \Box \ -77$

Order from least to greatest.

	a		b

25. –85, –56, 6, –6 _____   –3, –47, 80, –82 _____

26. 5, 10, –60, 99 _____   37, 76, 66, 73 _____

27. –7, 16, –47, –37 _____   –56, 97, 75, 61 _____

Mid-Test Chapters 1–4

Use the coordinate grid to answer the questions.

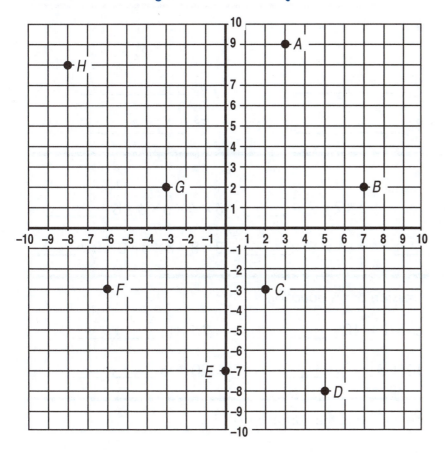

Write the ordered pair for each coordinate.

28. A _____

29. C _____

30. E _____

31. G _____

Name the point located at each ordered pair.

32. (–8, 8) _____

33. (–6, –3) _____

34. (5, –8) _____

35. (7, 2) _____

Mark the following points on the coordinate grid.

36. I at (–3, –5)

37. J at (4, –8)

38. K at (5, 2)

39. L at (–1, 6)

40. How many units is it from Point B to Point H? _____ units

41. How many units is it from Point F to Point D? _____ units

Check What You Know

Expressions and Equations

Write each power as a product of factors.

a	b	c

1. 2^4 _____ 9^2 _____ 5^3 _____

2. 4^2 _____ 8^5 _____ 7^3 _____

Use exponents to rewrite each expression.

3. $4 \times 4 \times 4 \times 4 =$ _____ $2 \times 2 \times 2 =$ _____ $6 \times 6 \times 6 \times 6 \times 6 =$ _____

4. $3 \times 3 \times 3 \times 3 \times 3 \times 3 \times 3 \times 3 =$ _____ $9 \times 9 \times 9 =$ _____ $8 \times 8 \times 8 \times 8 \times 8 \times 8 =$ _____

Identify each of the following as an *expression* or an *equation*.

5. $5 + x$ _____ $6 + 4 = 10$ _____ $75 \times n$ _____

6. $9 - 4 = 5$ _____ $10 + x$ _____ $20 \div 5$ _____

For each term below, identify the coefficient (C) and the variable (V).

7. $5y$ C ____ V ____ $2x$ C ____ V ____ n C ____ V ____

8. $12z$ C ____ V ____ $4m$ C ____ V ____ $9d$ C ____ V ____

Write the expression for each statement.

9. the product of 4 and the difference between 8 and 3 _____

10. 4 increased by the product of 5 and 3 _____

11. the difference between 16 and the product of 4 and 2 _____

12. the quotient of 25 and 5 increased by 3 _____

13. the product of 6 and 2 decreased by 1 _____

14. three times the quotient of 40 and 8 _____

15. 7 decreased by the product of 4 and 2 _____

Check What You Know

Expressions and Equations

Solve each equation.

	a	**b**	**c**
16.	$x - 4 = 4$ _____	$x + 3 = 5$ _____	$n - 2 = 0$ _____
17.	$b + 8 = 19$ _____	$n + 5 = 5$ _____	$y + 3 = 3$ _____
18.	$a + 4 = 11$ _____	$n - 8 = 8$ _____	$y - 5 = 5$ _____
19.	$\frac{a}{4} = 4$ _____	$a \times 4 = 4$ _____	$\frac{m}{5} = 5$ _____
20.	$y \times 20 = 30$ _____	$\frac{x}{12} = 3$ _____	$b \times 7 = 21$ _____
21.	$\frac{x}{5} = 20$ _____	$n \times 5 = 25$ _____	$\frac{x}{9} = 1$ _____

SHOW YOUR WORK

Solve the problems.

22. Eva spent $48 on a shirt and a pair of pants. The pants cost twice as much as the shirt. How much did each item cost?

Let s stand for the cost of the shirt.

Equation: _____ $s =$ _____

The shirt cost _____. The pants cost _____.

22.

23. In Ben's office, there are 5 more women than men. There are 23 women. How many men are there?

What is the unknown number? _____

Equation: _____ $n =$ _____

There are _____ men in the office.

23.

Lesson 5.1 Using Exponents

A **power** of a number represents repeated multiplication of the number by itself.
$10^3 = 10 \times 10 \times 10$ and is read 10 to the third power.

In **exponential** numbers, the **base** is the number that is multiplied, and the **exponent** represents the number of times the base is used as a factor. In 2^5, 2 is the base and 5 is the exponent.

2^5 means 2 is used as a factor 5 times.
$2 \times 2 \times 2 \times 2 \times 2 = 32$ $2^5 = 32$

Scientific notation for a number is expressed by writing the number as the product of a number between one and ten, and a power of ten.

3,000 can be written as $3 \times 1,000$ or 3×10^3.
3×10^3 is scientific notation for 3,000.

Some powers of 10 are shown in the table at right.

10^1	10	10
10^2	10×10	100
10^3	$10 \times 10 \times 10$	1,000
10^4	$10 \times 10 \times 10 \times 10$	10,000
10^5	$10 \times 10 \times 10 \times 10 \times 10$	100,000

Use the table above to write each number in scientific notation.

	a	b	c
1.	30 _____	4,000 _____	50,000 _____
2.	600,000 _____	700 _____	90 _____
3.	40,000 _____	100,000 _____	400 _____

Write each power as the product of factors.

4.	3^3 _____	5^5 _____	1^6 _____
5.	12^2 _____	8^3 _____	6^3 _____
6.	7^4 _____	4^4 _____	11^4 _____

Use exponents to rewrite each expression.

7.	$3 \times 3 \times 3$ _____	8×8 _____	$7 \times 7 \times 7 \times 7 \times 7$ _____
8.	24×24 _____	$4 \times 4 \times 4$ _____	$6 \times 6 \times 6 \times 6 \times 6 \times 6$ _____
9.	$2 \times 2 \times 2 \times 2$ _____	$38 \times 38 \times 38$ _____	$5 \times 5 \times 5 \times 5 \times 5$ _____

Evaluate each expression.

10.	a^4 if $a = 2$ _____	x^3 if $x = 4$ _____	n^7 if $n = 1$ _____
11.	n^2 if $n = 8$ _____	b^4 if $b = 3$ _____	x^3 if $x = 5$ _____
12.	a^5 if $a = 3$ _____	x^3 if $x = 6$ _____	n^2 if $n = 11$ _____

Lesson 5.1 Using Exponents

Write each power as the product of factors.

	a	b	c
1.	3^5 _____	9^3 _____	2^7 _____
2.	10^2 _____	3^4 _____	2^8 _____
3.	7^3 _____	4^2 _____	7^2 _____
4.	9^3 _____	8^1 _____	12^2 _____
5.	5^4 _____	11^3 _____	6^5 _____
6.	4^4 _____	10^3 _____	8^6 _____

Use exponents to rewrite each expression.

7. $3 \times 3 \times 3 =$ _____ $5 \times 5 \times 5 \times 5 \times 5 =$ _____ $2 \times 2 \times 2 \times 2 \times 2 \times 2 =$ _____

8. $9 \times 9 \times 9 =$ _____ $4 \times 4 \times 4 \times 4 \times 4 \times 4 \times 4 =$ _____ $21 \times 21 =$ _____

9. $10 \times 10 \times 10 \times 10 =$ _____ $8 \times 8 \times 8 \times 8 \times 8 =$ _____ $7 \times 7 \times 7 \times 7 =$ _____

Evaluate each expression.

10. 8^5 _____ 2^8 _____ 3^4 _____

11. 6^2 _____ 9^1 _____ 10^4 _____

12. 4^4 _____ 7^4 _____ 12^2 _____

Lesson 5.2 Parts of an Expression

A **variable** is a symbol, usually a letter of the alphabet, that stands for an unknown number, or quantity. a = variable

An **algebraic expression** is a combination of numbers, variables, and at least one operation. $x + 13$

A **term** is a number, variable, product, or quotient in an algebraic expression. In $3a + 5$, $3a$ is a term and 5 also is a term.

The term $3a$ means $3 \times a$. The number 3 is the coefficient of a. A **coefficient** is a number that multiplies a variable. In the expression $x + 5$, the coefficient of x is understood to be 1.

An **equation** is a sentence that contains an equal sign. $x + 13 = 25$

Identify each of the following as an *expression* or an *equation*.

	a	b	c
1.	$3 + x$ _____	$7 + 4 = 11$ _____	$55 \times n$ _____
2.	$x - 7 = 15$ _____	$b - 45$ _____	$24 = 6 \times 4$ _____

For each term below, identify the coefficient and the variable.

	a	b
3.	$3x$ coefficient _____ variable _____	$4y$ coefficient _____ variable _____
4.	z coefficient _____ variable _____	$5n$ coefficient _____ variable _____
5.	$7b$ coefficient _____ variable _____	m coefficient _____ variable _____
6.	r coefficient _____ variable _____	$6d$ coefficient _____ variable _____

Translate each phrase into an algebraic expression.

7. five more than n _____   eight decreased by x _____

8. x added to seven _____   the product of n and 11 _____

Translate each sentence into an equation.

9. Six times a number is 18. _____   Seventy less a number is 29. _____

10. Eight divided by a number is 2. _____   The product of 7 and 12 is 84. _____

Write the following expressions in words.

11. $6 - n = 3$ _____

12. $5 \times 13 = 65$ _____

Lesson 5.2 Parts of an Expression

Identify each of the following as an *expression* or an *equation*.

a	**b**	**c**
1. $8 + x$ _____	$9 + 7 = 16$ _____	$20 \times m = 60$ _____
2. $b \div 5$ _____	$32 = 8 \times 4$ _____	43×7 _____
3. $4h$ _____	$91 - 20 = 71$ _____	$17 + c$ _____
4. $36 = 9 \times 4$ _____	$65 - x$ _____	$30f$ _____

For each term below, identify the coefficient and the variable.

a	**b**
5. $6g$ coefficient _____ variable _____	p coefficient _____ variable _____
6. $5r$ coefficient _____ variable _____	$9t$ coefficient _____ variable _____
7. $2x$ coefficient _____ variable _____	$4n$ coefficient _____ variable _____
8. $3a$ coefficient _____ variable _____	$7d$ coefficient _____ variable _____
9. $20s$ coefficient _____ variable _____	y coefficient _____ variable _____

Translate each phrase into an expression or an equation.

10. the sum of 3 and b _____	8 times the sum of f and 7 _____
11. product of 8 and d _____	p added to 4 equals 9 _____
12. subtract 3 from 4 times m _____	r minus 2 is 8 _____
13. 4 times the sum of 5 and x _____	product of 10 and 2 _____
14. 12 times r minus 7 _____	the sum of 9 and k _____

Lesson 5.3   Writing Expressions

An **equation** is a number sentence that contains an equal sign.
An **expression** is a number phrase without an equal sign.
Equations and expressions may contain only numerals, or they also may contain variables. A **variable** is a symbol, usually a letter, that stands for an unknown number.

	Equation	Expression
Numerical	$3 \times 5 = 15$	$9 + 2$
Variable	$2n + 2 = 18$	$a - 5$

All equations and expressions express an idea.

3×4 means "three 4s." $6 \div 3 = 2$ means "6 divided by 3 is 2."

$n - 7$ means "n decreased by 7" or "a number decreased by 7."

$4n + 2 = 6$ means "four times a number, plus 2, is 6" or "4ns, plus 2, is 6."

Translate each phrase into an expression or an equation.

a

b

1. x increased by 5 _____   12 divided by a number _____

2. seven ns _____ c less than 7 _____

3. a number added to 15 is 23 _____   one-fourth of x _____

4. p added to 6 _____   the product of 15 and m _____

Translate each sentence into an equation. Use n for an unknown number.

5. 11 decreased by a number is 7. _____

6. 8 times a number, plus 4, is 84. _____

7. A number divided by 5 is 6. _____

Write each expression in words.

8. $n - 5$ _____

9. $3n \div 6$ _____

Lesson 5.3 Writing Expressions

Translate each phrase into an algebraic expression or an equation.

a   **b**

1. subtract 8 from 3 times d _____   take away 3 from x _____

2. g minus 2 is 14 _____ z is added to 8 _____

3. the sum of 7 and z _____   2 is subtracted from 4 times d _____

4. two-fifths of the sum of 6 and s _____ 9 minus c _____

5. 10 minus x _____   subtract 9 from the product of 4 and f _____

6. 3 is subtracted from 5 times a _____ y minus 3 is 15 _____

7. s is added to 9 _____   the sum of 8 and t _____

8. take away 9 from h _____   one-third of the sum of 7 and k _____

Write each expression in words.

9. $9 \div x$ _____

10. $3 \times g = 27$ _____

11. $6 \times m - 4$ _____

12. $\frac{1}{2} \times b + 9 = 11$ _____

13. $14 \div p$ _____

14. $6 \times b = 42$ _____

15. $9 \times d - 10$ _____

16. $\frac{1}{4} \times t + 8 = 16$ _____

Lesson 5.4 Equivalent Expressions

Equivalent expressions are created by simplifying values and combining terms.

$4(6x - 5) = 24x - 20$ Multiply each value by 4 to create an equivalent expression.

$3(4^3 + 7x) = 3(64 + 7x)$ First, calculate the value of the exponents.
$3(64 + 7x) = 192 + 21x$ Then, use the distributive property to create the equivalent expression.

$t + t + t = 3t$ Use multiplication in place of repeated addition.

Create expressions equivalent to the ones below.

1. $7(4z + 8b)$ _____

2. $8(2x + 3^2)$ _____

3. $4(r + r + r + r)$ _____

4. $9(3 + 8x)$ _____

5. $4^2(3 + 6t)$ _____

6. $\dfrac{t + t + t}{4}$ _____

7. $2(4s^3 + 2)$ _____

8. $30(3x + 4)$ _____

9. $6(5a + 9b)$ _____

10. $9(3x + 5^4)$ _____

11. $7(c + c + c)$ _____

12. $9(2 + 7f)$ _____

13. $7^5(4g - 8d)$ _____

14. $\dfrac{e + e + e}{5}$ _____

15. $5(3z^6 + 3)$ _____

16. $10(y + 2)$ _____

Lesson 5.4 Equivalent Expressions

Create expressions equivalent to the ones below.

1. $4(a + b)$ _____

2. $3(9a + 8b)$ _____

3. $9(x + 2y)$ _____

4. $2(9x + 3^2)$ _____

5. $5^3(2 + 4c)$ _____

6. $\frac{x + x}{3}$ _____

7. $4^2(12 + 5c)$ _____

8. $17(14r + 3^3) - 7r$ _____

9. $6(c - f)$ _____

10. $4(10b - 10c)$ _____

11. $8(g - 3d)$ _____

12. $3(7h + 4^2)$ _____

13. $4^5(3 + 5t)$ _____

14. $\frac{d + d}{10}$ _____

15. $6^4(25 + t)$ _____

16. $19(20f - w^4) + 3f$ _____

Lesson 5.5 Solving 1-Step Equations: Addition & Subtraction

Subtraction Property of Equality

If you subtract the same number from each side of an equation, the two sides remain equal.

$$x + 12 = 20$$

To undo the addition of 12, subtract 12.

$$x + 12 - 12 = 20 - 12$$
$$x + 0 = 8$$
$$x = 8$$

Addition Property of Equality

If you add the same number to each side of an equation, the two sides remain equal.

$$n - 3 = 15$$

To undo the subtraction of 3, add 3.

$$n - 3 + 3 = 15 + 3$$
$$n - 0 = 18$$
$$n = 18$$

Write the operation that would undo the operation in the equation.

	a	b
1.	$x - 4 = 3$ _____	$8 = b + 4$ _____
2.	$y + 7 = 25$ _____	$3 = a - 7$ _____

Solve each equation.

	a	b	c
3.	$a - 4 = 2$ _____	$y + 5 = 9$ _____	$x - 3 = 14$ _____
4.	$7 = x - 4$ _____	$b + 7 = 19$ _____	$y + 5 = 5$ _____
5.	$z - 7 = 5$ _____	$m - 5 = 5$ _____	$n + 1 = 1$ _____
6.	$x + 7 = 10$ _____	$x - 3 = 18$ _____	$x + 0 = 9$ _____
7.	$b + 4 = 4$ _____	$b - 8 = 12$ _____	$n + 8 = 12$ _____
8.	$z - 10 = 20$ _____	$z + 5 = 20$ _____	$x - 2 = 8$ _____

Write and solve the equation for each problem below.

9. Kelley went to the movies. She took 20 dollars with her. When she came home, she had 6 dollars. How much money did she spend? _____

9.

10. There are 27 students in Mrs. Yuen's homeroom. Twelve of them have home computers. How many students do not have home computers?

_____

10.

Lesson 5.5 Solving 1-Step Equations: Addition & Subtraction

Solve each equation.

	a	b	c
1.	$9 + d = 16$ _____	$y + 3 = 9$ _____	$12 + a = 27$ _____
2.	$18 - b = 4$ _____	$23 - c = 21$ _____	$w - 11 = 11$ _____
3.	$n + 8 = 41$ _____	$7 + m = 20$ _____	$9 + s = 9$ _____
4.	$t - 18 = 5$ _____	$36 - a = 36$ _____	$15 - b = 0$ _____
5.	$17 = c + 3$ _____	$29 = 5 + b$ _____	$36 = 35 + n$ _____
6.	$2 = d - 4$ _____	$19 = 25 - a$ _____	$12 = t - 12$ _____

Write an equation for each problem. Then, solve the equation.

7. Ruben read 37 pages in his history book over the weekend. He read 21 pages on Saturday. How many pages did he read on Sunday?

_____ He read _____ pages on Sunday.

8. The Garcias ate 9 pieces of toast for breakfast. If there are 33 slices of bread left, how many slices were in the loaf of bread?

_____ There were _____ slices in the loaf of bread.

9. In a 25-kilometer triathlon, competitors swim 2 kilometers, run 5 kilometers, and bike the rest. How far do they bike?

_____ They bike _____ kilometers.

Lesson 5.6 Solving 1-Step Equations: Multiplication & Division

Division Property of Equality

If you divide each side of an equation by the same nonzero number, the two sides remain equal.

$$3y = 21$$

To undo multiplication by 3, divide by 3.

$$\frac{3y}{3} = \frac{21}{3}$$
$$y = 7$$

Multiplication Property of Equality

If you multiply each side of an equation by the same number, the two sides remain equal.

$$\frac{a}{4} = 4$$

To undo division by 4, multiply by 4.

$$\frac{a}{4} \times \frac{4}{1} = 5 \times 4$$
$$a = 20$$

Write the operation that would undo the operation in each equation.

　　　　a

1. $5 \times n = 40$ _____

2. $\frac{x}{2} = 8$ _____

　　　　b

$\frac{y}{5} = 80$ _____

$a \times 7 = 42$ _____

Solve each equation.

　　　　　a　　　　　　　　　　　　　b　　　　　　　　　　　　　c

3. $3 \times a = 9$ _____　　　$\frac{x}{5} = 5$ _____　　　$\frac{n}{4} = 3$ _____

4. $\frac{x}{3} = 3$ _____　　　$n \times 4 = 4$ _____　　　$3 \times y = 24$ _____

5. $5 \times b = 10$ _____　　$\frac{b}{8} = 2$ _____　　　$4 \times a = 20$ _____

6. $\frac{m}{3} = 1$ _____　　　$8 \times n = 20$ _____　　$\frac{x}{5} = 2$ _____

7. $4 \times n = 1$ _____　　　$\frac{n}{4} = 5$ _____　　　$\frac{b}{3} = 27$ _____

8. $n \times 15 = 30$ _____　　$\frac{n}{4} = 10$ _____　　$n \times 12 = 36$ _____

9. $\frac{n}{18} = 2$ _____　　　$n \times 3 = 18$ _____　　$n \times 2 = 20$ _____

10. $\frac{n}{2} = 20$ _____　　$\frac{n}{16} = 1$ _____　　　$n \times 3 = 3$ _____

11. $5 \times b = 30$ _____　　$\frac{b}{5} = 30$ _____　　　$n \times 8 = 24$ _____

12. $\frac{n}{4} = 1$ _____　　　$\frac{b}{2} = 2$ _____　　　$n \times 6 = 48$ _____

Lesson 5.6 Solving 1-Step Equations: Multiplication & Division

Solve each equation.

	a	**b**	**c**
1.	$2 \times d = 18$ _____	$a \times 4 = 20$ _____	$5 \times n = 30$ _____
2.	$y \div 3 = 4$ _____	$t \div 9 = 3$ _____	$\frac{a}{5} = 3$ _____
3.	$8 \times s = 64$ _____	$p \times 16 = 16$ _____	$7 \times r = 42$ _____
4.	$\frac{n}{5} = 10$ _____	$n \div 3 = 12$ _____	$a \div 8 = 6$ _____
5.	$25 = 5 \times d$ _____	$0 = a \times 57$ _____	$32 = b \times 2$ _____
6.	$19 = \frac{x}{1}$ _____	$7 = b \div 4$ _____	$9 = \frac{c}{7}$ _____

Write an equation for each problem. Then, solve the equation.

7. Taryn practiced piano the same amount of time every day for 6 days. If she practiced a total of 12 hours, how many hours did she practice each day?

_____ She practiced _____ hours each day.

8. A group of friends decided to equally share a package of trading cards. If there were 48 cards in the package and each person received 12, how many friends were in the group?

_____ There were _____ friends in the group.

9. Twenty-five cars can take the ferry across the river at one time. If 150 cars took the ferry, and it was full each time, how many times did the ferry cross the river?

_____ The ferry crossed the river _____ times.

Lesson 5.7 Problem Solving

Write an equation to represent the problem, using the variable *n* for the unknown number. Then, solve for the value of the variable. Look at the following problem as an example.

Hanna bought some peaches. Kevin bought 12 peaches. He bought 2 times as many as Hanna. How many did Hanna buy?

What is the unknown number? <u>the number of peaches Hanna bought</u>

If *n* stands for that, what stands for the number of peaches Kevin bought? <u>2n</u>
What number is that? <u>12</u>

Equation: <u>2n = 12</u>   n = <u>6</u>

SHOW YOUR WORK

Solve each equation.

1. Jaden has a number of baseball cards. He has 35 more than his brother, who has 52. How many cards does Jaden have?

   What is the unknown number? _____

   Equation: _____   n = _____

   1.

2. Orlando paid $55.60 for a number of tickets to a hockey game. If each ticket was $6.95, how many tickets did Orlando buy?

   What is the unknown number? _____

   Equation: _____   n = _____

   2.

3. Erica's room is 1.5 times longer than it is wide. It is 18 feet long. How wide is it?

   What is the unknown number? _____

   Equation: _____   n = _____

   3.

4. In a recent basketball game, the Grizzlies lost by 11 points. The Palominos beat them with a score of 92 points. How many points did the Grizzlies score?

   What is the unknown number? _____

   Equation: _____   n = _____

   4.

Lesson 5.7 Problem Solving

Solve each problem.

1. Martha bought a soft drink for $3.00 and four candy bars. She spent a total of $11.00. How much did each candy bar cost?

   What is the unknown number? _____

   Equation: _____ n = _____

2. 248 students went on a trip to the zoo. All 6 buses were filled and 8 students had to travel in cars. How many students were in each bus?

   What is the unknown number? _____

   Equation: _____ n = _____

3. Todd sold half of his comic books and then bought 6 more. He now has 16. How many did he begin with?

   What is the unknown number? _____

   Equation: _____ n = _____

4. A bike shop charges $12.00, plus $6.00 an hour for renting a bike. Mike paid $48.00 to rent a bike. How many hours did he pay to have the bike checked out?

   What is the unknown number? _____

   Equation: _____ n = _____

5. Susan spent $8 of her allowance going to the movies. She gave the dog a bath and earned $5.00. What is her weekly allowance if she ended up with $20.00?

   What is the unknown number? _____

   Equation: _____ n = _____

1.

2.

3.

4.

5.

Lesson 5.8 Solving Inequalities

Inequalities can be solved the same way that equations are solved.

$6 + q > 14$

$6 + q - 6 > 14 - 6$

$q > 8$

1. Subtract 6 from both sides of the inequality to isolate the variable on one side of the inequality.

2. The variable q represents a value that is greater than 8.

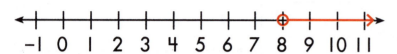

A number line can be used to represent the possible values of the variable. An open circle shows that the values do not include 8. For inequalities that use $\leq$ or $\geq$, a closed circle indicates that the values do include that point.

Solve the inequalities and represent the possible values of the variable on a number line.

1. $6 > z - 2$

2. $g + 7 < -12$

3. $d - 5 < 7$

4. $15 > k + 2$

5. $1 + x > -16$

6. $y + 8 < -9$

7. $8 \leq 8 + r$

8. $w + 8 \geq 11$

Lesson 5.8 Solving Inequalities

Solve the inequalities and represent the possible values of the variable on a number line.

1. $x - 2 < 12$

2. $-1 + y > 17$

3. $p + 2 < -13$

4. $-7 + v < -17$

5. $6 + s \geq -6$

6. $f + 2 \geq 8$

7. $-10 > w - 1$

8. $-3 + g \leq 9$

Sometimes word problems contain dependent and independent variables. The **dependent variable** in a problem is the value that is affected by the other values in the problem. The **independent variable** is the value that affects the outcome of the dependent variable.

If a car has to travel 200 miles, the speed (s) the car is driving is the independent variable and the time (t) it takes to make the trip is the dependent variable. This can be represented by the formula, $200 = s \times t$, and can be solved by creating a table.

Dependent Variable	Time	5 hours	4 hours	$3\frac{1}{3}$ hours
Independent Variable	Speed	40 miles/hr.	50 miles/hr.	60 miles/hr.

Use tables to identify the variables and find possible solutions to the problems.

1. Maria has to buy apples at the grocery store. Apples cost $1.25 per pound. How much will Maria spend on apples?

   What equation will you use? _____

Dependent Variable				
Independent Variable				

2. When a tree is planted, it is 6 feet tall. Each month, it grows by 2 feet. How tall will it get over time?

   What equation will you use? _____

_____ Variable	Height			
_____ Variable	Time	3 months	6 months	2 years

Lesson 5.9 Dependent and Independent Variables

Use tables to identify the variables and find possible solutions to the problems.

1. Students have been assigned to read a book that is 150 pages. Every student reads at a different speed. Depending on reading speed, how many days will it take different students to read the assigned book?

Write the equation: _____

_____ **Variable**	Time (Days)			
_____ **Variable**	Reading Speed	15 pages/ day	20 pages/ day	30 pages/ day

2. As a candle burns, it decreases in height by 2 inches every hour. If the candle is 12 inches tall when it is lit, how will the height change over time?

Write the equation: _____

Dependent Variable	Height (inches)			
Independent Variable	Time (hours)			

3. As a daffodil grows, it increases in height by 3 inches every 2 days. If the daffodil plant starts at 1 inch on day one, how will the height change over time?

Write the equation: _____

Dependent Variable				
Independent Variable				

4. The temperature in an oven increases by 8° every minute. If the starting temperature of the oven is 250, how will the temperature change over time?

Write the equation: _____

_____ **Variable**				
_____ **Variable**				

NAME _____

Check What You Learned

Expressions and Equations

CHAPTER 5 POSTTEST

Write each power as a product of factors.

	a	b	c
1.	3^5 _____	12^2 _____	6^4 _____
2.	5^4 _____	7^3 _____	8^5 _____
3.	4^5 _____	2^9 _____	9^3 _____

Use exponents to rewrite each expression.

4. $2 \times 2 \times 2 \times 2 \times 2 =$ _____ $8 \times 8 \times 8 =$ _____ $25 \times 25 =$ _____

5. $4 \times 4 \times 4 =$ _____ $5 \times 5 \times 5 \times 5 \times 5 \times 5 \times 5 \times 5 =$ _____ $15 \times 15 \times 15 =$ _____

Identify each of the following as an *expression* or an *equation*.

6. $7 + x$ _____ $9 + 4 = 13$ _____ $85 \times n$ _____

7. $10 - 6 = 4$ _____ $12v$ _____ $18 - g$ _____

For each term below, identify the coefficient (C) and the variable (V).

8. $9y$ C ____ V ____ $4b$ C ____ V ____ m C ____ V ____

Write the expression for each statement.

9. the product of 2 and the difference between 7 and 3   _____

10. 3 increased by the product of 4 and 2   _____

11. the difference between 12 and the product of 4 and 3   _____

12. the quotient of 20 and 5 increased by 16   _____

13. the product of 7 and 2 divided by 3   _____

14. twice the quotient of 45 and 9   _____

15. the difference between 15 and the product of 4 and 2   _____

16. triple the sum of 16 and 9   _____

Spectrum Math
Grade 6
96

Check What You Learned
Chapter 5

Check What You Learned

Expressions and Equations

Solve each equation.

a	b	c
17. $x - 5 = 3$ _____	$x + 5 = 8$ _____	$y - 4 = 0$ _____
18. $x - 19 = 8$ _____	$x - 12 = 4$ _____	$n + 8 = 8$ _____
19. $b - 7 = 0$ _____	$n + 3 = 3$ _____	$x + 2 = 8$ _____
20. $\frac{x}{3} = 3$ _____	$n \times 5 = 5$ _____	$\frac{b}{2} = 1$ _____
21. $b \times 8 = 12$ _____	$\frac{x}{3} = 3$ _____	$a \times 2 = 3$ _____
22. $\frac{n}{4} = 4$ _____	$n \times 8 = 8$ _____	$b \times 3 = 18$ _____

Solve each problem.

23. Patrick paid $72.60 for some computer games. Each game cost $24.20. How many games did Patrick buy?

What is the unknown number? _____

Equation: _____ $n =$ _____

23.

24. Noelle and Gina have a combined height of 130 inches. Noelle is 4 inches taller than Gina. How tall is each girl?

Let n stand for Noelle's height.

Equation: _____

Noelle is _____ inches tall.

Gina is _____ inches tall.

24.

NAME _____

Check What You Know

Geometry

Find the area or surface area of each figure.

a	b	c

1.

8 in.   60 in.

5 m   75 m

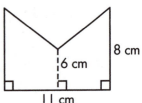

8 cm   6 cm   11 cm

$A =$ _____ sq. in.

$A =$ _____ sq. m

$A =$ _____ sq. cm

2.

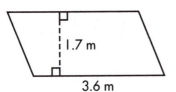

1.7 m   3.6 m

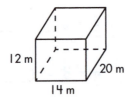

12 m   20 m   14 m

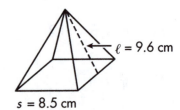

$\ell = 9.6$ cm $s = 8.5$ cm

$A =$ _____ sq. m

$SA =$ _____ sq. m

$SA =$ _____ sq. cm

Find the volume of each rectangular solid.

a	b	c

3.

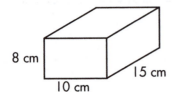

8 cm   10 cm   15 cm

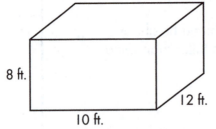

8 ft.   10 ft.   12 ft.

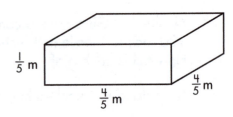

$\frac{1}{5}$ m $\frac{4}{5}$ m $\frac{4}{5}$ m

$V =$ _____ cu. cm

$V =$ _____ cu. ft.

$V =$ _____ cu. m

NAME _____

Check What You Know

Geometry

Use the coordinate grids to find the missing vertex of each polygon.

a **b**

4. a rectangle with points at (4, −3), (4, −6), and (−3, −6)

a right triangle with points at (−3, 2) and (4, −5)

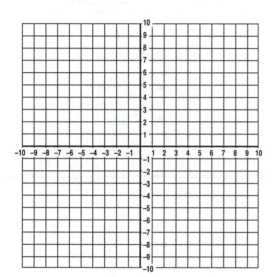

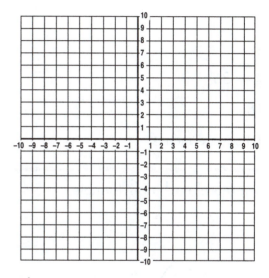

The missing point is at _____.

The missing point is at _____ or _____.

SHOW YOUR WORK

Solve each problem.

5. The sail on a boat is shaped like a right triangle. Its base is 15 feet and its height is 22 feet. What is the area?

The area is _____ square feet.

6. A shoe box is 6 inches wide, 10 inches long, and 5 inches high. What is the volume?

The volume is _____ cubic inches.

7. A ski jump is shaped like a right triangle. Its base is 27 feet long and the highest point on the ramp is 4 feet. What is the area of the ski jump?

The area is _____ square feet.

5.

6.

7.

Lesson 6.1 Calculating Area: Triangles

The area (A) of a triangle is one-half the of the base (b) times the height (h).

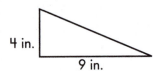

$$A = \frac{1}{2} \times b \times h$$

or

$$A = \frac{1}{2}bh$$

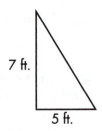

$A = \frac{1}{2} \times 9 \times 4$

$\quad = \frac{1}{2} \times 36$

$\quad = 18$

$A = 18$ square inches

$A = \frac{1}{2} \times 5 \times 7$

$\quad = \frac{1}{2} \times 35$

$\quad = 17\frac{1}{2}$

$A = 17\frac{1}{2}$ square feet

Find the area of each right triangle.

a   **b**

1.

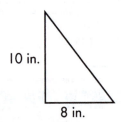

$A =$ _____ sq. in.

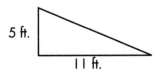

$A =$ _____ sq. ft.

2.

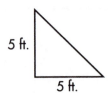

$A =$ _____ sq. ft.

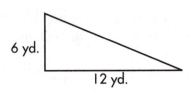

$A =$ _____ sq. yd.

Lesson 6.1 Calculating Area: Triangles

The area of a triangle is related to the area of a rectangle.

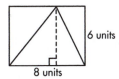

The dashed line indicates the height of the triangle.

rectangle: $A = 8 \times 6 = 48$ sq. units

triangle: $A = \frac{1}{2}(8)(6) = 24$ sq. units

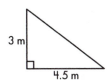

$A = \frac{1}{2}(4.5)(3) = 6\frac{3}{4}$ sq. m

Notice that in a right triangle the height is the length of one of the legs. This is not the case with acute and obtuse triangles.

Find the area of each triangle below.

a	b	c

1.

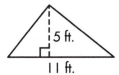

$A =$ _____ sq. ft.

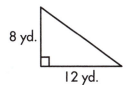

$A =$ _____ sq. yd.

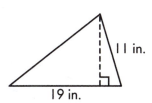

$A =$ _____ sq. in.

2.

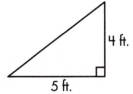

$A =$ _____ sq. ft.

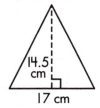

$A =$ _____ sq. cm

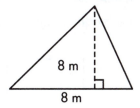

$A =$ _____ sq. m

Lesson 6.2 Calculating Area: Quadrilaterals

Area is the number of square units it takes to cover a figure. To find the **area of a rectangle**, multiply the length by the width. $A = lw$

7 units

2 units

$A = 7 \times 2$
$A = 14$ square units

8 units

$A = s \times s = 8 \times 8$
$A = 64$ square units

Find the area of each rectangle below.

          a   **b**   **c**

1.

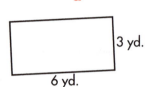
3 yd.

6 yd.

18 m

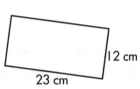
12 cm

23 cm

$A =$ _____ sq. yd.

$A =$ _____ sq. m

$A =$ _____ sq. cm

2.

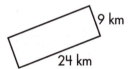
9 km

24 km

23 in.

8 ft.

6 ft.

$A =$ _____ sq. km

$A =$ _____ sq. in.

$A =$ _____ sq. ft.

Find the length of each rectangle below.

3.

6 in.

4.5 ft.

9 m

$A = 54$ sq. in.

$\ell =$ _____ in.

$A = 58.5$ sq. ft.

$\ell =$ _____ ft.

$A = 81$ sq. m

$\ell =$ _____ m

Lesson 6.2 Calculating Area: Quadrilaterals

A parallelogram is a polygon with 2 sets of parallel sides. To find the **area of a parallelogram**, multiply the measure of its base by the measure of its height: $A = b \times h$ or $A = bh$.

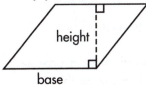

$b = 8$ in. and $h = 7$ in. What is A?

$A = b \times h$ $A = 8 \times 7 = 56$ in.^{2} or 56 square inches.

Find the area of each parallelogram.

a	b	c

1.

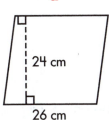

24 cm

26 cm

$A = $ _____ sq. cm

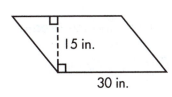

15 in.

30 in.

$A = $ _____ sq. in.

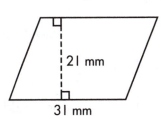

21 mm

31 mm

$A = $ _____ sq. mm

2.

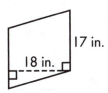

17 in.

18 in.

$A = $ _____ sq. in.

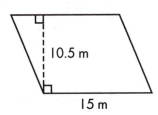

10.5 m

15 m

$A = $ _____ sq. m

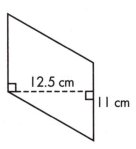

12.5 cm

11 cm

$A = $ _____ sq. cm

Lesson 6.3   Calculating Area: Other Polygons

To find the area of an irregular shape, separate the shape into its component figures and find the area of each one.

This figure can be divided into two rectangles, as shown by the dotted line.

To find the missing side measurement of shape A, look at the vertical measurements you already know: 10 mm and 7 mm. Because the missing side must be the difference between 10 and 7, subtract to get the answer: $10 - 7 = 3$ mm.

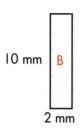

To find the area of shape A, multiply $l \times w$.
$$3 \times 3 = 9 \text{ mm}$$

Follow the same steps to find the area of shape B.
$$5 - 3 = 2 \text{ mm}$$
$$A = 10 \times 2 = 20 \text{ mm}$$

Then, add the two areas together to get the area of the entire irregular shape.
$$9 + 20 = 29 \text{ square mm}$$

Find the area of each figure.

	a	b	c

1.

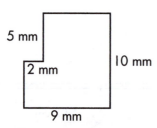

A = _____ sq. mm

10 yd.

8 yd.   8 yd.

3 yd.

A = _____ sq. yd.

8 cm

4 cm   3 cm
              2 cm

A = _____ sq. cm

2.

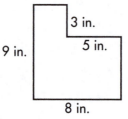

A = _____ sq. in.

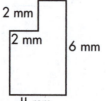

A = _____ sq. mm

2 mm

4 mm   4 mm

9 mm

A = _____ sq. mm

Lesson 6.3 Calculating Area: Other Polygons

Some irregular shapes are made up of more than one type of figure.

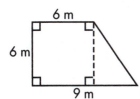

This figure can be divided into a square and a triangle.

area of square	area of triangle
$A = 6 \times 6 = 36$	$A = \frac{1}{2} \times 3 \times 6 = 9$

The area of the figure is $36 + 9 = 45$ square meters.

Find the area of each figure.

	a	b	c
1.	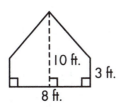	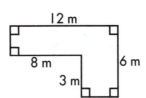	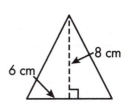
	$A = $ _____ sq. ft.	$A = $ _____ sq. m	$A = $ _____ sq. cm

2.	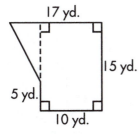	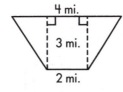	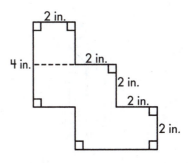
	$A = $ _____ sq. yd.	$A = $ _____ sq. mi.	$A = $ _____ sq. in.

Lesson 6.4 Volume of Rectangular Solids

The **volume** (V) of a rectangular solid is the product of the measure of its length (ℓ), the measure of its width (w), and the measure of its height (h). $V = ℓ \times w \times h$

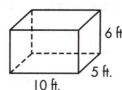

$V = 10 \times 5 \times 6$
$= 50 \times 6$
$= 300$
The volume is 300 cubic feet.

Find the volume of each rectangular solid.

| | a | b | c |

1.

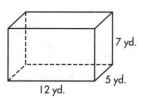

$V =$ _____ cu. yd.

$V =$ _____ cu. in.

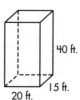

$V =$ _____ cu. ft.

2.

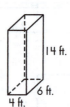

$V =$ _____ cu. ft.

$V =$ _____ cu. in.

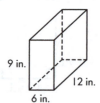

$V =$ _____ cu. in.

Lesson 6.4 Volume of Rectangular Solids

Find the volume of each rectangular solid.

a	b	c

1.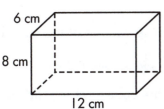

V = _____ cu. cm

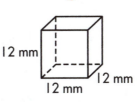

V = _____ cu. mm

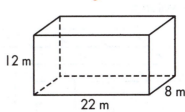

V = _____ cu. m

2.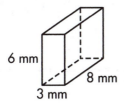

V = _____ cu. mm

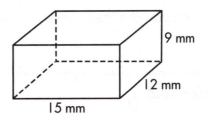

V = _____ cu. mm

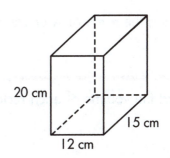

V = _____ cu. cm

3.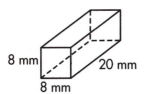

V = _____ cu. mm

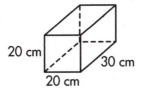

V = _____ cu. cm

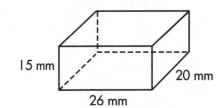

V = _____ cu. mm

NAME _____

Volume of Rectangular Solids

The volume of a rectangular solid with fractional edge lengths can also be measured by packing the solid with cubes that share a common denominator with the edge lengths. In this rectangular solid, each side length has a denominator of 5, so the solid can be packed with $\frac{1}{5}$ inch cubes to determine its volume.

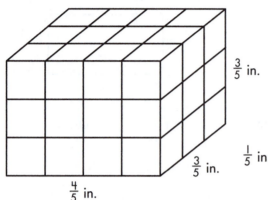

First, calculate the volume of the cube itself.

$$\frac{1}{5} \times \frac{1}{5} \times \frac{1}{5} = \frac{1}{125} \text{ cubic inches}$$

Next, add up the cubes in the solid. You can see from the top layer that there are 12 cubes per layer, and $12 \times 3 = 36$.

Last, multiply the number of cubes times the volume of one cube.

$$36 \times \frac{1}{125} = \frac{36}{125} \text{ cubic inches}$$

This is the same answer you get when you use the formula $l \times w \times h$. $\frac{4}{5} \times \frac{3}{5} \times \frac{3}{5} = \frac{36}{125}$

Find the volume of each rectangular solid.

        a   **b**

1.

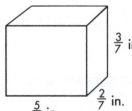

$\frac{3}{7}$ in.
$\frac{2}{7}$ in.
$\frac{5}{7}$ in.

$V =$ _____ cu. in.

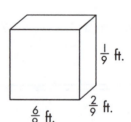

$\frac{1}{9}$ ft.
$\frac{2}{9}$ ft.
$\frac{6}{9}$ ft.

$V =$ _____ cu. ft.

2.

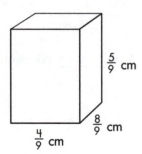

$\frac{5}{9}$ cm
$\frac{8}{9}$ cm
$\frac{4}{9}$ cm

$V =$ _____ cu. cm

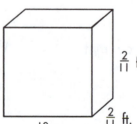

$\frac{2}{11}$ ft.
$\frac{2}{11}$ ft.
$\frac{10}{11}$ ft.

$V =$ _____ cu. ft.

Lesson 6.5 Problem Solving

Solve each problem.

1. Mr. Ruiz's vase is 3 inches long, 2 inches wide, and 9 inches tall. What is the volume of the vase?

   The volume of the vase is _____ cubic inches.

2. Andrew has an aquarium that is 16 inches long, 10 inches wide, and 9 inches deep. What is the volume of Andrew's aquarium?

   The volume of Andrew's aquarium is _____ cubic inches.

3. A city park is shaped like a right triangle. Its base is 20 yards and its depth is 48 yards. What is the area of the park?

   The area of the park is _____ square yards.

4. A paving brick is 3 inches wide, 2 inches high, and 6 inches long. What is the volume of the brick?

   The volume is _____ cubic inches.

5. A tabletop is shaped like a right triangle with a base of 25 inches and a depth of 30 inches. What is the area of the tabletop?

   The area of the tabletop is _____ square inches.

6. A rectangular playground is 90 yards long and 40 yards wide. What is the area of the playground?

   The area of the playground is _____ square yards.

1.

2.

3.

4.

5.

6.

Lesson 6.5 Problem Solving

Solve each problem.

1. Craig's backyard is a rectangle 25 meters long and 20 meters wide. What is the area of Craig's yard?

   The area of Craig's yard is _____ square meters.

   1.

2. A shipping crate is 0.85 meters long, 0.4 meters wide, and 0.3 meters high. What is the volume of the crate?

   The crate's volume is _____ cubic meters.

   2.

3. A rectangular poster is 45 centimeters long and 28 centimeters wide. What is the area of the poster?

   The poster's area is _____ square centimeters.

   3.

4. A room is 8.6 meters wide and 10.2 meters long. What is the area of the room?

   The area of the room is _____ square meters.

   4.

5. Megan's jewelry box is 25 centimeters long, 12 centimeters wide, and 10 centimeters high. What is the volume of Megan's jewelry box?

   The volume of Megan's jewelry box is _____ cubic centimeters.

   5.

6. A rectangular CD jewel case is approximately 14 centimeters long and 12 centimeters wide. What is the area of the CD jewel case?

   The area of the jewel case is _____ square centimeters.

   6.

Lesson 6.6 Surface Area: Rectangular Solids

The **surface area** of a solid is the sum of the areas of all surfaces of the solid. A rectangular solid has 6 surfaces.

The area of each surface is determined by finding:

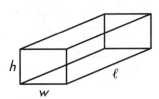

length × width, length × height, width × height

The total surface area is found using this formula:

$SA = 2\ell w + 2\ell h + 2wh$

If $\ell = 10$ m, $w = 6$ m, and $h = 4$ m, the surface area is found as follows:

$SA = 2(10 \times 6) + 2(10 \times 4) + 2(6 \times 4)$

$SA = 2(60) + 2(40) + 2(24) = 120 + 80 + 48 = 248$ m^2

Find the surface area of each rectangular solid.

a	b	c

1.

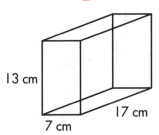

13 cm 17 cm 7 cm

SA = _____ cm^2

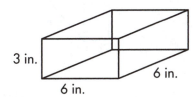

3 in. 6 in. 6 in.

SA = _____ in.^{2}

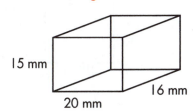

15 mm 20 mm 16 mm

SA = _____ mm^2

2.

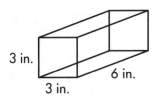

3 in. 6 in. 3 in.

SA = _____ in.^{2}

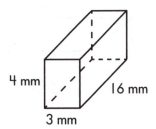

4 mm 16 mm 3 mm

SA = _____ ft.^{2}

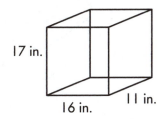

17 in. 16 in. 11 in.

SA = _____ in.^{2}

Lesson 6.6 Surface Area: Rectangular Solids

Find the surface area of each rectangular solid.

	a	**b**	**c**

1.

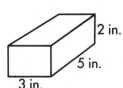 2 in. 5 in. 3 in.

SA = _____ sq. in.

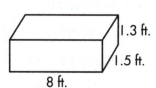 1.3 ft. 1.5 ft. 8 ft.

SA = _____ sq. ft.

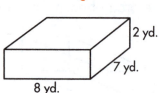 2 yd. 7 yd. 8 yd.

SA = _____ sq. yd.

2.

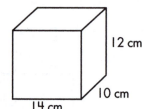 12 cm 10 cm 14 cm

SA = _____ sq. cm

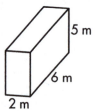 5 m 6 m 2 m

SA = _____ sq. m

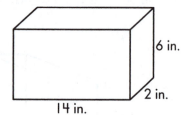 6 in. 2 in. 14 in.

SA = _____ sq. in.

3.

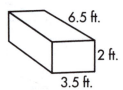 6.5 ft. 2 ft. 3.5 ft.

SA = _____ sq. ft.

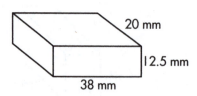 20 mm 12.5 mm 38 mm

SA = _____ sq. mm

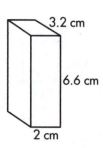 3.2 cm 6.6 cm 2 cm

SA = _____ sq. cm

Lesson 6.7 Surface Area: Pyramids

The **surface area** of a solid is the sum of the areas of all surfaces of the solid. The surface area of a square pyramid is the sum of the area of the square base and each of the 4 triangular sides.

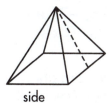

side

slant height, or *length* (ℓ) of the side

Each triangle's area is $\frac{1}{2}$ base × height. In a pyramid, **base** refers to the side length and **height** refers to the slant height, or length. So surface area or $SA = (\text{side} \times \text{side}) + 4(\frac{1}{2} \text{ side} \times \text{length})$.

$SA = s^2 + 2s\ell$ SA is given in **square units**, or **units²**.

If $s = 6$ cm and $\ell = 10$ cm, what is the surface area?

$SA = s^2 + 2s\ell$

$SA = 6^2 + 2 \times 6 \times 10 = 36 + 120 = 156 \text{ cm}^2$

Find the surface area of each square pyramid.

	a	**b**	**c**

1.

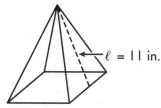

$\ell = 11$ in.
$s = 8$ in.
$SA =$ _____ in.²

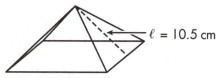

$\ell = 10.5$ cm
$s = 15$ cm
$SA =$ _____ cm²

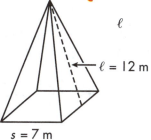

ℓ
$\ell = 12$ m
$s = 7$ m
$SA =$ _____ m²

2.

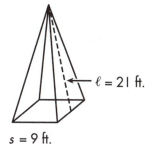

$\ell = 21$ ft.
$s = 9$ ft.
$SA =$ _____ ft.²

$\ell = 8$ cm
$s = 10$ cm
$SA =$ _____ cm²

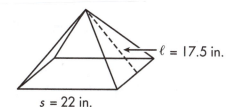

$\ell = 17.5$ in.
$s = 22$ in.
$SA =$ _____ in.²

Lesson 6.8 Graphing Polygons: Rectangles

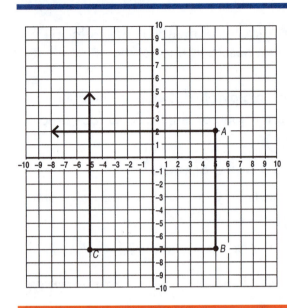

Coordinate planes can help you solve problems with polygons, such as rectangles.

If points A (5, 2), B (5, −7), and C (−5, −7) are vertices of a rectangle, where does vertex D fall?

Connect the vertices and then draw lines straight from points A and C to find where vertex D will fall.

Point D occurs at point (−5, 2).

Use the coordinate grids to find the missing vertex of each polygon.

1. a rectangle with points at (0, 2), (−6, 2), and (−6, 4)

   The missing point is at _____.

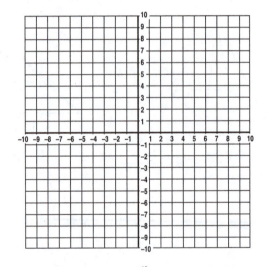

2. a rectangle with points at (3, −4), (3, 5), and (−2, 5)

   The missing point is at _____.

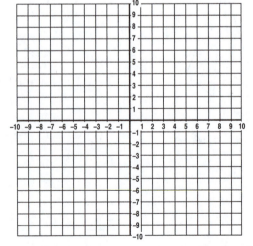

Chapter 6, Lesson 8
Geometry

Lesson 6.9 Graphing Polygons: Right Triangles

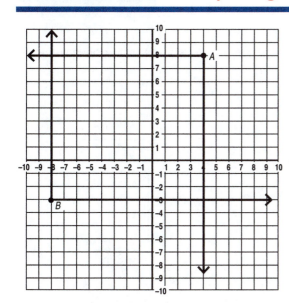

Triangle problems can also be solved through graphing on the coordinate plane.

If points A (4, 8) and B (−8, −3) are vertices of the hypotenuse (longest side) of a right triangle, where does vertex C fall?

Connect the vertices and then draw lines straight from points A and B to find where vertex C will fall.

Point C can occur at point (−8, 8) or point (4, −3).

Use the coordinate grids to find the missing vertex of each polygon.

1. a right triangle with points at (3, 2) and (−5, 6)

The missing point is at _____
or _____.

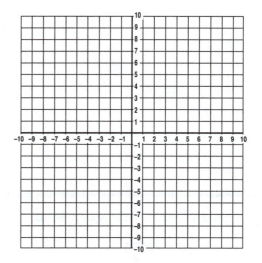

2. a right triangle with points at (−4, −6) and (5, 2)

The missing point is at _____
or _____.

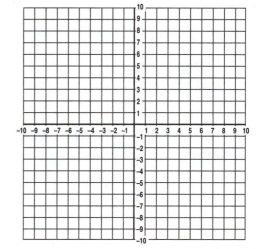

Check What You Learned

Geometry

Find the area or surface area of each figure.

a	**b**	**c**

1.

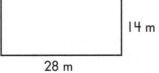

14 m

28 m

A = _____ sq. in.

15 in.

42 in.

A = _____ sq. cm

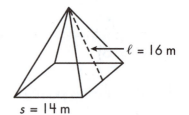

4 in.

6 in. 10 in.

8 in.

A = _____ sq. in

2.

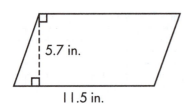

5.7 in.

11.5 in.

A = _____ sq. in.

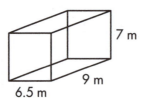

7 m

9 m

6.5 m

SA = _____ sq. m

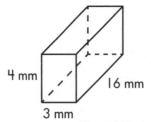

ℓ = 16 m

s = 14 m

SA = _____ sq. m

Find the volume of each rectangular solid.

3.

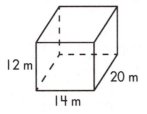

12 m

20 m

14 m

V = _____ cu. m

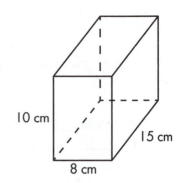

4 mm

16 mm

3 mm

V = _____ cu. mm

10 cm

15 cm

8 cm

V = _____ cu. cm

CHAPTER 6 POSTTEST

NAME _____

Check What You Learned

Geometry

Use the coordinate grids to find the missing vertex of each polygon.

a

4. a rectangle with points at (5, 2), (−2, 2), and (5, −4)

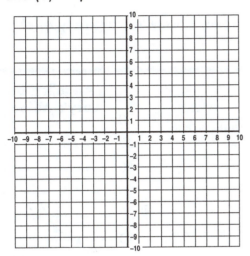

The missing point is at _____.

b

a right triangle with points at (−1, 3) and (2, 3)

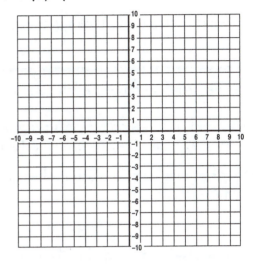

The missing point is at _____ or _____.

SHOW YOUR WORK

Solve each problem.

5. A piece of metal is shaped like a right triangle. Its base is 18 feet and its height is 24 feet. What is its area?

The area is _____ square feet.

5.

6. Stephanie's hamster cage is 20 inches long, 12 inches wide, and 10 inches deep. What is the volume of the cage?

The volume is _____ cubic inches.

6.

7. Pablo's snake cage is 30 inches long, 15 inches wide, and 12 inches deep. What is the volume of the cage?

The volume of the cage is _____ cubic inches.

What is the volume of the cage in cubic feet?

The volume of the cage is _____ cubic feet.

7.

Spectrum Math
Grade 6

Check What You Learned
Chapter 6

NAME _____

Check What You Know

Probability and Statistics

Circle the statistical questions below.

	a	b

1. How often do students in my class text?   What is my favorite subject?

2. How many classes do I take in a day?   What are my classmates' favorite types of candy?

Use the line graph to answer each question.

Angelica and Lucy are on a fitness program. They are keeping track of how far they walk. They record their totals after each week.

3. After two weeks, how much farther did Lucy walk than Angelica? _____

4. During what week did Angelica not walk? _____

5. Who walked farthest during the 6 weeks? _____

6. How much farther did she walk? _____

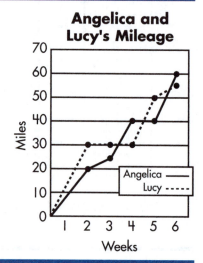

Angelica and Lucy's Mileage

Angelica ———
Lucy ------

Draw a stem-and-leaf plot for each set of numbers.

7. 25, 18, 36, 24, 31, 56, and 72

8. 16, 15, 41, 21, 23, 32, 30, 23, 26, and 26

Check What You Know

Probability and Statistics

Find the mean, median, mode, and range of each set of numbers.

9. 97, 82, 66, 98, 66, 85, 82, 66, and 78

mean: _____   mode: _____

median: _____   range: _____

10. 8, 14, 6, 12, 12, 12, 20

mean: _____   mode: _____

median: _____   range: _____

Use the histogram to answer the questions.

11. In which range did most exam scores fall?

_____

12. In which range did the fewest scores fall?

_____

13. If 59 or less is a failing score, how many students failed the exam?

_____

14. How many more students passed than failed?

_____

15. How many students took the exam?

_____

16. Did more or less than half the class pass the exam? _____

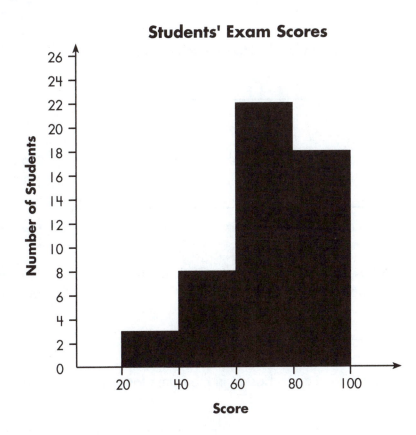

Students' Exam Scores

Lesson 7.1 Asking Statistical Questions

A **statistical question** has answers that will vary.

"How old are students in my school?" is a statistical question because not every answer will be the same.

"How old am I?" is not a statistical question because there is only one answer.

Read each question and write *statistical* or *not*.

a	b
1. How tall are the students in my class?	What does this apple cost?
_____	_____
2. What grades did students score on the test?	How fast can dogs run 100 yards?
_____	_____
3. How many marbles are in the jar?	Does a chocolate bar weigh more than a pack of jelly beans?
_____	_____
4. What was the difference in rainfall between March and April?	How many miles can cars travel on a gallon of gas?
_____	_____
5. Will I score a basket in the game tonight?	How often do adults eat breakfast?
_____	_____

Lesson 7.1 Asking Statistical Questions

Write one statistical question for each category below.

1. height of students

_____

2. test scores

_____

3. number of pages in books

_____

4. number of students in classes

_____

5. price of apples

_____

6. type of automobile

_____

7. exercise

_____

Lesson 7.2   Describing Data

Data can be described by how the values relate to each other and how they are spread out.

10, 7, 8, 8, 23, 45, 77, 90, 90

The data is spread over 82 points.

The center value of the data is 23.

The lowest value in the data is 7.

All of the values are greater than 0.

The highest value in the data is 90.

8 and 90 appear twice each in the data.

Write three descriptions of each data set.

1. 62, 68, 63, 67, 69, 63, 67

A. _____

B. _____

C. _____

2. 0, 0, 2, 8, 6, 10, 100

A. _____

B. _____

C. _____

3. 0, 8, 20, 45, 84, 92, 45

A. _____

B. _____

C. _____

Lesson 7.2 Describing Data

Write three descriptions of each data set.

1. 7.3, 6.7, 6.6, 5.7, 5.4, 5.4, 6.4

A. _____

B. _____

C. _____

2. 2, 5, 9, 3, 5, 4, 7, 9, 0

A. _____

B. _____

C. _____

3. 7, 4, 5, 3, 9, 6, 2, 9, 3, 4, 3

A. _____

B. _____

C. _____

Lesson 7.3   Measures of Center: Mean

The **mean** of a data set is computed by adding all of the numbers in the data together and dividing by the number of values contained in the data set.

84, 66, 102, 114, 78, 90

84 + 66 + 102 + 114 + 78 + 90 = 534

$$\begin{array}{r} 89 \\ 6\overline{)534} \end{array}$$

89

1. Add all of the values in the data set together.

2. Divide the sum by the number of values in the data set.

3. The mean of the data set is 89.

Find the mean of each data set.

a	b

1. 48, 64, 80, 48   85, 75, 90, 60, 80

_____   _____

2. 84, 140, 105, 119, 105, 84, 105   102, 78, 114, 96, 96, 102

_____   _____

3. 119, 140, 119, 91, 91, 126, 91   96, 108, 78, 96, 72, 102

_____   _____

4. 52, 52, 64, 80   55, 90, 70, 90, 85

_____   _____

5. 112, 140, 77, 126, 91, 77, 133   90, 84, 72, 102, 84, 66

_____   _____

6. 99, 89, 46, 97, 17, 75   60, 31, 24, 50, 44, 88

_____   _____

Lesson 7.4 Measures of Center: Median

The **median** of a data set is the middle number when the values are placed in order from least to greatest. If there are an even number of values in the data set, the median is the average of the two middle terms.

35, 29, 26, 37, 21, 38, 38

21, 26, 29, 35, 37, 38, 38   1. Put the data in order from least to greatest.

——————→ 35 ←————   2. Count in from the outside to find the middle value.

35   3. The median of this data set is 35.

Find the median of each data set.

                  a   b

1. 23, 31, 32, 34, 39, 38, 38, 34, 38   24, 20, 28, 19, 18, 11, 19, 18, 19

_____   _____

2. 19, 11, 28, 13, 23, 14, 28   3, 9, 6, 2, 1, 10, 1, 2, 1

_____   _____

3. 26, 34, 24, 37, 36, 22, 34, 26, 34   10, 2, 3, 4, 6, 7, 6

_____   _____

4. 23, 32, 38, 40, 30, 34, 23   15, 21, 23, 16, 19, 14, 23, 14, 23

_____   _____

5. 10, 3, 5, 1, 7, 8, 5, 1, 5   51, 87, 77, 93, 67, 81, 77, 93, 77

_____   _____

6. 78, 35, 85, 93, 62, 95, 88, 51, 45   97, 64, 25, 26, 8, 24, 36, 72, 56

_____   _____

Lesson 7.5 Measures of Center: Mode

The **mode** of a data set is the value that occurs the most often. Sometimes a data set has more than one mode.

2, 6, 1, 8, 10, 3, 10, 1, 10

1, 1, 2, 3, 6, 8, 10, 10, 10   1. Put the data in order from least to greatest.

(1, 1) 2, 3, 6, 8, 10, (10, 10)   2. Look for values that occur more than once.

10   3. The value that occurs the most times is the mode.

Find the mode for each data set.

a	b
1. 3, 2, 8, 5, 1, 4, 4, 3, 4	39, 25, 40, 38, 22, 37, 40
_____	_____
2. 24, 16, 26, 12, 28, 23, 28, 26, 28	118, 115, 108, 124, 106, 120, 108
_____	_____
3. 16, 18, 12, 15, 21, 26, 26	32, 28, 22, 36, 24, 35, 24, 32, 24
_____	_____
4. 253, 295, 204, 151, 118, 277, 277	22, 16, 14, 15, 25, 21, 21
_____	_____
5. 95, 73, 55, 69, 72, 65, 73, 72, 73	3, 8, 4, 2, 7, 10, 4
_____	_____
6. 14, 93, 14, 96, 13, 5, 84, 69, 93	92, 44, 32, 82, 86, 59, 22, 32
_____	_____

Lesson 7.6 Finding Measures of Center

The **mean** is the average of a set of numbers. To find the mean, add all the numbers and divide by the number of values in the set.

The **median** is the middle number of a data set. If there are two middle numbers, the median is the average of the two.

The **mode** is the number that appears most often in a data set.

Example: 12, 15, 18, 23, 8, 10, and 12
Mean: $12 + 15 + 18 + 23 + 8 + 10 + 12 = 98$ $\frac{98}{7} = 14$

To find the median, arrange the numbers in order.   8, 10, 12, <u>12</u>, 15, 18, 23
Median: 12   Mode: 12

Find the mean, median, and mode of each data set. Show your work.

	a	**b**

1. 32, 35, 25, 43, 43   8, 12, 23, 12, 15

mean _____   mean _____

median _____   median _____

mode _____   mode _____

2. 10, 18, 12, 14, 12, 12   17, 15, 15, 28, 20, 26

mean _____   mean _____

median _____   median _____

mode _____   mode _____

3. 52, 61, 79, 78, 56, 79, 71   37, 50, 67, 83, 34, 49, 37

mean _____   mean _____

median _____   median _____

mode _____   mode _____

Lesson 7.7 Using Measures of Center

Measures of center can be used to describe a data set. Each measure of center allows for different observations about the set.

The **mean** is the most popular measure of center. It is the average, so it provides the clearest picture of the center of the data, but only if there are no outliers (values that are far away from the majority of the numbers in the set).

The **median** is the most useful measure when the data set contains outliers.

The **mode** is the most useful measure when the values in the data set are non-numerical.

Tell which measure of center would be best for describing each data set.

a	b
1. 3, 4, 5, 5, 7, 6, 21	62, 65, 72, 68, 66
_____	_____
2. 54, 72, 85, 67, 93, 85, 61, 89	red, blue, green, red, blue, yellow, blue
_____	_____
3. $14.60, $7.25, $15.70, $15.25, $14.90	8, 25, 19, 19, 25, 9, 9, 18, 25, 9, 8, 7, 10
_____	_____
4. 0, 1, 3, 5, 5, 5, 7, 9, 9, 11, 15, 99	A, B, C, A, B, C, D, A, B, B
_____	_____

Lesson 7.7 Using Measures of Center

Find the measures of center for each data set and decide which would be best to describe the data set.

	a		**b**

1. Cesar's Test Scores: 84, 80, 78, 90, 76, 88, 86, 80, 94

Which is the best measure of center? _____

mean: _____

median: _____

mode: _____

2. Basketball Team Scores: 78, 77, 81, 84, 67, 78, 75, 42

Which is the best measure of center? _____

mean: _____

median: _____

mode: _____

3. Daily Theater Attendance: 124, 127, 111, 119, 107, 99, 115

Which is the best measure of center? _____

mean: _____

median: _____

mode: _____

4. Marisa's Daily Tips: $15, $21, $18, $13, $52, $21, $25

Which is the best measure of center? _____

mean: _____

median: _____

mode: _____

Lesson 7.8 Measures of Variability: Range

The **range** of a data set is the difference between the largest value and smallest value contained in the data set.

11, 12, 15, 15, 13, 12

11, 12, 12, 13, 15, 15   1. Put the data set in order from least to greatest.

11, 12, 12, 13, 15, 15   2. Find the largest value and smallest value.

15 − 11 =   3. Subtract.

4   4. The range of this data set is 4.

Find the range of each data set.

	a	b
1.	11, 10, 12, 9	79, 79, 79, 84
2.	25, 30, 32, 23, 27, 22	96, 94, 101, 96, 91, 92
3.	36, 33, 37, 37, 41, 33	506, 508, 510, 509
4.	277, 280, 287, 276	10, 8, 9, 12, 6, 8
5.	12, 9, 16, 9	95, 92, 89, 97, 94, 88

Lesson 7.9 Measures of Variability: Interquartile Range

The **interquartile range** (IQR) of a data set is the difference between the median of the lower half of a data set and the median of the upper half of the same data set.

13, 15, 9, 35, 25, 17, 19

9, 13, 15, 17, 19, 25, 35   1. Put the data set in order from least to greatest.

9, 13, 15   17   19, 25, 35   2. Find the lower half, median, and upper half of the data set.

Q1=13   Q3=25   3. Find the medians of the lower half and upper half.

25 − 13 =   4. Subtract.

12   5. The interquartile range of the data set is 12.

Find the interquartile range for each set of data.

a   b

1. 6, 1, 3, 8, 5, 11, 1, 5   80, 90, 95, 85, 70

median: _____   median: _____

Q1: _____   Q1: _____

Q3: _____   Q3: _____

IQR: _____   IQR: _____

2. 70, 75, 90, 100, 95   45, 43, 13, 11, 5, 2

median: _____   median: _____

Q1: _____   Q1: _____

Q3: _____   Q3: _____

IQR: _____   IQR: _____

3. 45, 39, 17, 16, 4, 1   29, 58, 15, 75, 22, 16, 64

median: _____   median: _____

Q1: _____   Q1: _____

Q3: _____   Q3: _____

IQR: _____   IQR: _____

Lesson 7.10 Measures of Variability: Mean Absolute Deviation

The **mean absolute deviation** (MAD) of a data set is a value that shows if the data set is consistent. The closer the mean absolute deviation of a data set to zero, the more consistent it is.

17, 19, 8, 32, 21, 24, 19

8, 17, 19, 19, 21, 24, 32   1. Put the data set in order from least to greatest.

Mean = 20   2. Find the mean of the data set.

12, 3, 1, 1, 1, 4, 12   3. Find the absolute value of the difference between the mean
                                   and each value in the set.
                                   (For example, $20 - 8 = 12$; $|12| = 12$)

Mean = 8.71   4. Find the mean of those absolute values.

MAD = 8.71   5. The mean absolute deviation of this data set is 8.71. This tells
                                   us that the values in the set are on average about 8.71 away
                                   from the middle.

Find the mean absolute deviation of each data set. Round each answer to two decimal places.

a   b

1. 10, 16, 18, 15, 15, 10, 23   41, 56, 38, 45, 55, 51, 52

    mean: _____   mean: _____

    value differences: value differences:

    _____   _____

    MAD: _____   MAD: _____

2. 10, 12, 18, 25, 25, 11, 22   22, 33, 44, 55, 66, 88, 55, 55, 11, 22

    mean: _____   mean: _____

    value differences: value differences:

    _____   _____

    MAD: _____   MAD: _____

Lesson 7.11 Using Measures of Variability

The **range** of a data set is the difference between the largest value and smallest value contained in the data set.

The **interquartile range** (IQR) of a data set is the difference between the median of the lower half of a data set and the median of the upper half of the same data set.

The **mean absolute deviation** (MAD) of a data set is a value that helps understand if the data set is consistent. If the mean absolute deviation of a data set is close to zero, the data set is more consistent.

Complete the table by listing the measures of variability for each data set. Round answers to two decimal places.

Data	Range	IQR	MAD
1. 43, 48, 80, 53, 59, 65, 58, 66, 70, 50, 76, 62	_____	_____	_____
2. 12, 47, 26, 25, 38, 45, 35, 35, 41, 39, 32, 25, 18, 30	_____	_____	_____
3. 99, 45, 23, 67, 45, 91, 82, 78, 62, 51	_____	_____	_____
4. 10, 2, 5, 6, 7, 3, 4	_____	_____	_____
5. 23, 56, 45, 65, 59, 55, 61, 54, 85, 25	_____	_____	_____
6. 55, 63, 88, 97, 58, 90, 88, 71, 65, 77, 75, 88, 95, 86	_____	_____	_____

Lesson 7.12 Plotting Data: Stem-and-Leaf Plots

A set of data can be organized into a **stem-and-leaf plot** by using place values.

87, 38, 35, 76, 48, 57, 68, 44, 63, 49, 63, 64, 71

The tens digits are the stems and the ones digits are the leaves.

Stem	Leaves
3	5 8
4	4 8 9
5	7
6	3 3 4 8
7	1 6
8	7

This allows you to see the least (35), the largest (87), the range (52), the median (63), and the mode (63).

Key: 3 | 5 = 35

Create a stem-and-leaf plot for each set of data. Include a key for each plot.

a

b

1. 14, 31, 34, 21, 13, 28, 33

63, 38, 72, 54, 50, 79, 64, 39, 57, 49

2. 48, 38, 34, 25, 27, 37, 49

88, 96, 99, 75, 87, 93, 81, 84, 91, 73

3. 19, 25, 38, 17, 24, 33, 13

26, 37, 25, 33, 35, 46, 27, 45, 23, 41

Lesson 7.13 Plotting Data: Box-and-Whisker Plots

Box-and-whisker plots are helpful in interpreting the distribution of data.
For example, the results of a test might include these 15 scores:

66, 56, 75, 77, 98, 72, 48, 83, 73, 89, 65, 74, 87, 85, 81

The numbers should be arranged in order:

48, 56, 65, 66, 72, 73, 74, 75, 77, 81, 83, 85, 87, 89, 98

The median is 75. The **lower quartile** is the median of the lower half (66). The **upper quartile** is the median of the upper half (85). Draw a box around the median with its ends going through the quartiles. Each quartile contains one-fourth of the scores.

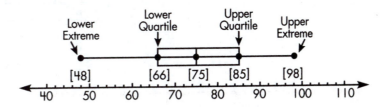

Answer the questions using the box-and-whisker plot above.

1. Half of the students scored higher than _____ on the test.

2. _____ scores are represented in the box part of the plot.

3. The range of the scores on the test is _____.

The scores on a recent daily quiz were 10, 15, 20, 20, 30, 30, and 40.

4. What is the median of these scores? _____

5. What is the lower quartile? _____

6. What is the upper quartile? _____

7. Using the number line below, draw a box-and-whisker plot for these scores.

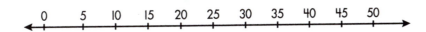

Lesson 7.14 Plotting Data: Line Graphs

Mrs. Martin's homeroom and Mr. Lopez's homeroom had a canned food drive. The **line graph** shows how many cans were collected after each day.

On Monday, how many more cans did Mr. Lopez's class collect than Mrs. Martin's class?

Mr. Lopez's class collected ___5___ more cans than Mrs. Martin's class on Monday.

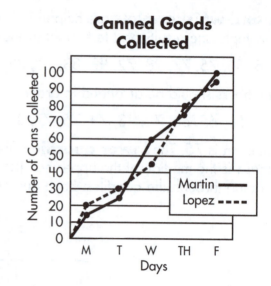

Canned Goods Collected

Use the line graph above to answer the following questions

1. On Monday, whose homeroom collected the most cans? _____

2. By Tuesday, how many cans had Mr. Lopez's homeroom collected? _____

3. On which day was the difference between the number of cans collected by each homeroom the greatest? _____

4. Which homeroom collected the most cans on that day? _____

5. How many cans total had been collected by both homerooms by Tuesday? _____

6. On what day did Mrs. Martin's homeroom bring in the most cans? _____

7. On what day did Mr. Lopez's homeroom bring in the most cans? _____

8. On what day did Mrs. Martin's homeroom bring in the least number of cans? _____

9. By Wednesday, how many cans had been collected by both homerooms? _____

10. How many cans were collected by both homerooms during the week? _____

Lesson 7.15 Plotting Data: Histograms

A **histogram** displays data using bars of different heights. It is different from a bar graph because it shows data grouped into ranges. Both axes of a histogram should be numerical.

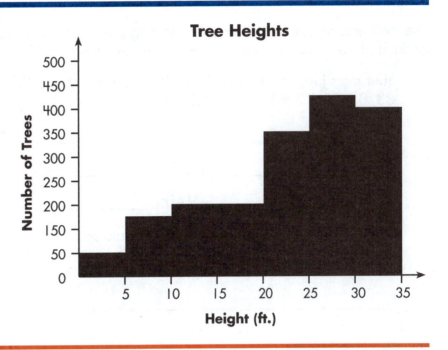

Tree Heights

Number of Trees (y-axis: 0, 50, 150, 200, 250, 300, 350, 400, 450, 500)

Height (ft.) (x-axis: 5, 10, 15, 20, 25, 30, 35)

Use the histogram above to answer the following questions.

1. How many trees were measured in all? _____

2. In what range did the most trees fall? _____

3. In what range did the least trees fall? _____

4. What percentage of trees were less than 20 feet tall? _____

5. What percentage of trees were greater than 20 feet tall? _____

6. How many more trees were 30–35 feet tall than 20–25 feet tall? _____

7. What is the range of heights shown? _____

8. Predict how many trees would be in the 35–40 foot range if it were included on the graph. _____

9. Explain the basis for your prediction.

   _____

10. Draw a star above the bar where a tree that measures 21 feet would be included.

Lesson 7.16 Summarizing Data Sets

Use measures of center and variability to help summarize these data sets. Round answers to two decimal places. Plot the data using a stem-and-leaf plot to show how the data is spread.

1. Your class just took a science test. These are the scores: 97, 99, 81, 78, 34, 96, 63, 100, 85, 83, 85, 88, 79, 82, 94, 85, 83, and 72.

   mode: _____   range: _____

   median: _____   IQR: _____

   mean: _____   MAD: _____

   Write 2 to 3 sentences that describe this data set.

   _____

   _____

   _____

   _____

Stem	Leaves

2. The soccer team at Wilson Middle School played ten games this year. They scored 4, 3, 1, 5, 3, 2, 5, 3, 2, and 4 goals in their games.

   mode: _____   range: _____

   median: _____   IQR: _____

   mean: _____   MAD: _____

   Write 2 to 3 sentences that describe this data set.

   _____

   _____

   _____

   _____

Stem	Leaves

Lesson 7.16 Summarizing Data Sets

Use measures of center and variability to help summarize these data sets. Round answers to two decimal places. Then, plot the data using a box-and-whisker plot to show how the data is spread.

1. The height of twelve 6th graders is collected in inches. Their heights are 60, 54, 48, 64, 52, 50, 68, 64, 58, 56, 56, and 64.

   mode: _____   Box-and-Whisker Plot

   median: _____

   mean: _____

   range: _____

   IQR: _____

   MAD: _____

   Write 2 to 3 sentences that describe this data set.

   _____

   _____

2. A teacher decides to collect information on how long students spend doing homework each evening. She talks to 15 students and receives this data (in minutes): 30, 15, 60, 45, 15, 45, 45, 60, 75, 30, 45, 30, 45, 15, and 45.

   mode: _____   Box-and-Whisker Plot

   median: _____

   mean: _____

   range: _____

   IQR: _____

   MAD: _____

   Write 2 to 3 sentences that describe this data set.

   _____

   _____

Lesson 7.16 Summarizing Data Sets

Use measures of center and variability to help summarize this data set. Round answers to two decimal places. Then, plot the data using a line graph to show how the data is spread.

A school keeps track of how many students are buying notebooks each month from the school store. They collected this information.

Month	Notebooks Sold
Jan.	25
Feb.	30
Mar.	15
Apr.	20
May	15
June	5
July	0
Aug.	35
Sept.	20
Oct.	15
Nov.	20
Dec.	30

mode: _____

median: _____

mean: _____

range: _____

IQR: _____

MAD: _____

Write 2 to 3 sentences that describe this data set.

_____

_____

Check What You Learned

Probability and Statistics

Write a statistical question for each category.

1. age _____

2. saving money _____

Use the set of data below to complete the following.

38, 25, 22, 18, 12, 36, 31, 22

3. Draw a stem-and leaf plot to show how this data is distributed.

4. Draw a box-and-whisker plot to show how this data is distributed.

Find the measures of center and variability for each set of data. Circle the best measure of center for describing the data set.

5. 9, 15, 7, 13, 13, 13, 21

mean: _____   range: _____

median: _____   IQR: _____

mode: _____   MAD: _____

Check What You Learned

Probability and Statistics

Find the measures of center and variability for each set of data. Circle the best measure of center for describing the data set.

6. 45, 38, 52, 47, 33, 54, 47, 39, 41

mean: _____   range: _____

median: _____   IQR: _____

mode: _____   MAD: _____

Use the data below to complete the following.

Renee's parents are going to buy a new car. To help them choose an environmentally-friendly car, Renee recorded the gas mileage of their top 10 choices. She used letters for the cars so her parents wouldn't be biased. Use her data to complete a histogram showing the range of gas mileages.

Car	Gas Mileage (mpg)
A	19
B	14
C	21
D	38
E	8
F	36
G	26
H	18
I	16
J	28

7.

8. How many cars are they considering that get fewer than 20 miles per gallon? _____

9. How many cars are they considering that get more than 20 miles per gallon? _____

10. In what range do the most cars fall? _____

Final Test   Chapters 1–7

Multiply or divide.

	a	b	c	d
1.	248 × 32	432 × 218	0.68 × 8.9	10.65 × 2.31

2. $24\overline{)5482}$ $17\overline{)45820}$ $0.89\overline{)3.84}$ $3.5\overline{)9.52}$

3. $\frac{1}{8} \times \frac{3}{5} =$ $\frac{2}{3} \times \frac{3}{7} =$ $3\frac{1}{7} \times \frac{5}{8} =$ $2\frac{1}{3} \times \frac{13}{8} =$

4. $\frac{6}{7} \div \frac{1}{2} =$ $\frac{3}{5} \div \frac{7}{10} =$ $\frac{5}{8} \div \frac{1}{3} =$ $1\frac{2}{3} \div \frac{3}{5} =$

Complete the chart with the equivalent decimals, percents, and fractions.

	a Percent	b Decimal	Fraction		c Percent	Decimal	d Fraction
5.	25%	_____	_____		_____%	.44	_____
6.	110%	_____	_____		_____%	.98	_____
7.	73%	_____	_____		_____%	.65	_____

Solve each ratio.

	a	b	c
8.	$\frac{3}{5} = \frac{\square}{20}$ _____	$\frac{\square}{6} = \frac{12}{18}$ _____	$\frac{4}{\square} = \frac{10}{20}$ _____
9.	$\frac{5}{8} = \frac{15}{\square}$ _____	$\frac{8}{25} = \frac{\square}{100}$ _____	$\frac{12}{\square} = \frac{1}{3}$ _____

Final Test Chapters 1–7

Compare the integers using <, >, or =.

	a	b	c	d	e	f
10.	$-12 \boxed{} -30$	$82 \boxed{} 17$	$-21 \boxed{} -57$	$-29 \boxed{} -45$	$-57 \boxed{} 15$	$15 \boxed{} -69$

Write each power as a product of factors.

	a	b	c
11.	4^2 _____	15^3 _____	2^6 _____

Use exponents to rewrite each expression.

12. $5 \times 5 \times 5 =$ _____ $6 \times 6 \times 6 \times 6 \times 6 =$ _____ $12 \times 12 \times 12 \times 12 =$ _____

Write the expression for each statement.

13. the quotient of 24 and the difference between 8 and 4 _____

14. the sum of 6 and the product of 4 and 7 _____

Plot the given coordinates on the grid. Then, answer the questions.

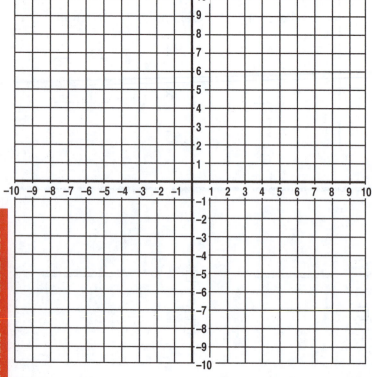

15. A (–3, 7)

16. B (3, –3)

17. C (–8, –6)

18. D (4, –6)

19. E (–10, 5)

20. How many units is it from Point A to Point E? _____ units

21. How many units is it from Point B to Point C? _____ units

22. How many units is it from Point D to Point E? _____ units

Spectrum Math
Grade 6
144

CHAPTERS 1–7 FINAL TEST

Final Test
Chapters 1–7

Final Test Chapters 1–7

Create expressions equivalent to the ones below.

	a	**b**
23.	$3 \times (4 + 2) =$ _____	$(5 \times 2) - (3 \times 2) =$ _____
24.	$(6 \times 8) + (6 \times 4) =$ _____	$8 \times (7 - 4) =$ _____

Solve each inequality or equation.

	a	**b**	**c**
25.	$23 - c < 6$ _____	$d + 11 > 15$ _____	$28 = a + 9$ _____
26.	$8 \times b = 48$ _____	$p - 13 = 5$ _____	$n \div 8 = 5$ _____

Use a table to identify the variables and find possible solutions to the problem.

27. Joy has to get from her house to the park, which is 10 miles away. If she walks, she can go 4 miles per hour. If she rides her bike, she can go 10 miles per hour. And, if she rides in a car she can travel at 40 miles per hour. How long will it take her to get to the park?

What equation will you use? _____

Dependent Variable				
Independent Variable				

Use the coordinate grid to find the missing vertex of each polygon.

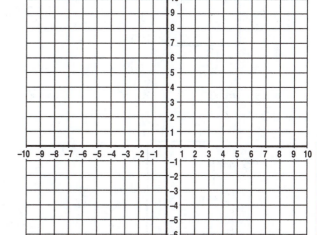

28. a rectangle with points at (4, 6), (–2, 6), and (–2, 1)

The missing point is at _____.

29. a right triangle with points at (4, 0) and (10, –4)

The missing point is at _____ or _____.

Spectrum Math
Grade 6

Final Test
Chapters 1–7
145

CHAPTERS 1–7 FINAL TEST

Final Test Chapters 1–7

Find the area, surface area, or volume of each figure.

a	b	c

30.

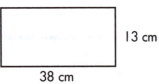

$A =$ _____ sq. cm

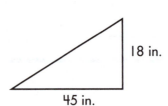

$A =$ _____ sq. in.

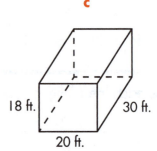

$V =$ _____ cu. ft.

31.

$A =$ _____ sq. cm

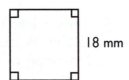

$A =$ _____ sq. mm

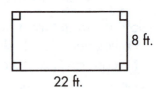

$A =$ _____ sq. ft.

32.

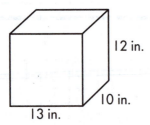

$SA =$ _____ sq. in.

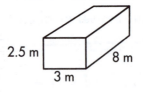

$V =$ _____ cu. m

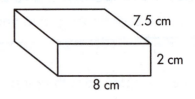

$SA =$ _____ sq. cm

33.

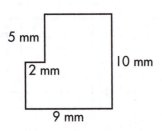

$A =$ _____ sq. mm

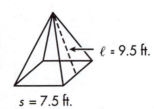

$SA =$ _____ sq. ft.

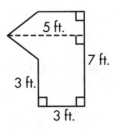

$A =$ _____ sq. ft.

CHAPTERS 1–7 FINAL TEST

Final Test Chapters 1–7

Use this data set to complete the following.

Points scored on quiz: 9, 18, 12, 9, 13, 22, 8, 23, 16, 17, 22, 20, 22, 15, 10, 17, 21, 23, 14, 11

34. Make a stem-and-leaf plot of the data.

35. Complete the histogram.

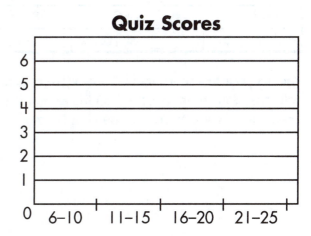

Quiz Scores

36. Find the measures of center and variability for the data.

mean: _____   range: _____

median: _____   IQR: _____

mode: _____   MAD: _____

37. What percentage of the people scored 16–20 points? _____%

38. What was the highest number of points scored on the quiz? _____

39. What was the lowest number of points scored on the quiz? _____

40. What percentage of the scores range from 21 to 25 points? _____%

Spectrum Math
Grade 6

CHAPTERS 1–7 FINAL TEST

Final Test
Chapters 1–7
147

Scoring Record for Posttests, Mid-Test, and Final Test

Chapter Posttest	Your Score	Performance			
		Excellent	Very Good	Fair	Needs Improvement
1	_____ of 36	32–36	29–31	25–28	24 or fewer
2	_____ of 39	35–39	31–34	27–30	26 or fewer
3	_____ of 48	43–48	38–42	33–37	32 or fewer
4	_____ of 44	39–44	35–38	31–34	30 or fewer
5	_____ of 59	53–59	47–52	41–46	40 or fewer
6	_____ of 16	14–16	12–13	10–11	9 or fewer
7	_____ of 20	18–20	16–17	14–15	13 or fewer
Mid-Test	_____ of 98	88–98	78–87	69–77	68 or fewer
Final Test	_____ of 105	95–105	84–94	74–83	73 or fewer

Record your test score in the Your Score column. See where you score falls in the Performance columns. Your score is based on the total number of required responses. If your score is fair or needs improvement, review the chapter material.

Grade 6 Answers

Chapter 1

Pretest, page 5

	a	b
1.	(4 × 6) + (4 × 2)	2 × (5 + 4)
2.	(4 × 2) + (4 × 6)	(6 × 5) − (6 × 1)
3.	6 × (6 − 3)	(8 × 3) − (8 × 1)

	a	b	c
4.	5	12	12
5.	13	19	16
6.	12	30	28
7.	210	12	105

Pretest, page 6

	a	b	c	d
8.	82,056	137,388	471,960	1,183,572
9.	86	152 R31	2,026	1,163 R13
10.	0.858	0.3526	$1,256.48	$27.99
11.	800	2,420	2.65	$0.55
12.	23			
13.	140			

Lesson 1.1, page 7

	a	b
1.	Commutative	Associative
2.	Identity	Commutative
3.	Associative	Property of Zero
4.	Identity	Commutative
5.	3 + (5 + 2)	7 × 5
6.	4	(3 × 2) × 5
7.	9 + 7	2 + (5 + 4)
8.	7	37
9.	0	0

Lesson 1.2, page 8

	a	b
1.	multiply	add
2.	add	multiply
3.	(4 × 6) + (4 × 2)	2 × (5 + 4)
4.	5 × (1 + 6)	(4 × 2) + (4 × 6)
5.	(8 × 4) + (8 × 3)	5 × (0 + 1)
6.	5	2
7.	6	5
8.	2	4
9.	16	16
10.	21	25

Lesson 1.2, page 9

- **1a.** (22 × 100) + (22 × 2) = 2,244
- **1b.** (40 × 25) − (1 × 25) = 975
- **2a.** (146 × 30) + (146 × 3) = 4,818
- **2b.** (30 × 16) − (2 × 16) = 448
- **3a.** (30 × 35) + (6 × 35) = 1,260
- **3b.** (50 × 106) + (1 × 106) = 5,406
- **4a.** (20 × 256) − (1 × 256) = 4,864
- **4b.** (40 × 17) + (5 × 17) = 765
- **5a.** (57 × 40) − (57 × 2) = 2,166
- **5b.** (48 × 40) + (48 × 5) = 2,160
- **6a.** (80 × 80) + (2 × 80) = 6,560
- **6b.** (50 × 82) + (1 × 82) = 4,182
- **7a.** (40 × 142) + (3 × 142) = 6,106
- **7b.** (264 × 70) − (264 × 3) = 17,688

- **8a.** (10 × 39) + (2 × 39) = 468
- **8b.** (60 × 35) − (2 × 35) = 2,030

Lesson 1.3, page 10

	a	b	c	d
1.	8,748	13,056	11,220	49,795
2.	113,300	86,184	227,664	284,886
3.	331,364	471,534	342,042	440,295
4.	747,612	901,550	955,192	2,070,672

Lesson 1.4, page 11

	a	b	c	d	e
1.	5 r4	2 r14	4	4 r2	2 r14
2.	2 r2	7	27 r1	32	29 r14
3.	30 r5	13 r23	19 r25	26 r17	18

Lesson 1.4, page 12

	a	b	c	d	e
1.	110 r25	312	369 r21	179 r2	110
2.	154 r20	113	270 r2	523	225
3.	1,467 r1	725	828 r40	886	569

Lesson 1.5, page 13

	a	b	c	d
1.	8,624	14,340	71,687	13,888
2.	10,615	16,399	52,125	90,396
3.	138	359	83	151
4.	318	158	117	694

Lesson 1.6, page 14

1.	540; 60	3.	560; 80	5.	40; 10
2.	40; 30; 1,200	4.	300; 90; 27,000	6.	690; 230

Lesson 1.7, page 15

1.	1, 2, 4, 8	1, 2, 4	4
	1, 2, 3, 4, 6, 12		
2.	1, 2, 3, 6	1, 2, 3, 6	6
	1, 2, 3, 6, 9, 18		
3.	1, 2, 3, 4, 6, 8, 12, 24	1, 3	3
	1, 3, 5, 15		
4.	1, 2, 4	1, 2	2
	1, 2, 3, 6		
5.	1, 5	1	1
	1, 2, 3, 4, 6, 12		
6.	1, 2, 4, 8, 16	1, 2, 4	4
	1, 2, 3, 4, 6, 12		

Lesson 1.7, page 16

	a	b			a	b
1.	1	3	5.	2	11
2.	14	9	6.	26	4
3.	12	5	7.	3	16
4.	18	7	8.	5	9

Lesson 1.8, page 17

	a	b			a	b
1.	306	1976	5.	224	48
2.	1728	260	6.	405	630
3.	4290	126	7.	21624	14620
4.	92	75			

Grade 6 Answers

Lesson 1.8, page 18

	a	b			a	b
1.	130	805		5.	132	135
2.	2655	2255		6.	684	168
3.	4828	4788		7.	325	4851
4.	140	200		8.	135	216

Lesson 1.9, page 19

	a	b	c	d	e
1.	5.6	0.04	0.0975	13.44	17.5
2.	0.0918	0.0486	28.105	2.1087	275.04
3.	19.8468	206.703	303.986	20.4102	563.85
4.	95.934	58.734	15.036	2.2382	0.6724
5.	0.1698	9.434	0.1909	0.09	12.532

Lesson 1.10, page 20

	a	b	c	d
1.	2.2	85	0.4	1.5
2.	40	5.3	40	65
3.	3000	30	0.25	1.2
4.	0.4	40	5	6

Lesson 1.11, page 21

1.	20.8 lb.	3.	0.465 lb.	5.	$54.48	7.	21.6
2.	15	4.	372	6.	300		

Lesson 1.11, page 22

1.	0.347	3.	$4.02	5.	$22.42	7.	0.705
2.	$25.12	4.	115.84	6.	1.433		

Posttest, page 23

	a	b
1.	$(3 \times 5) - (3 \times 2)$	$(5 + 8) \times 2$
2.	$(7 \times 7) - (7 \times 4)$	$7 \times (6 - 3)$
3.	$(3 \times 8) + 3 \times 2$	$(5 \times 9) - (5 \times 4)$

	a	b	c
4.	4	6	2
5.	4	1	2
6.	30	15	20
7.	60	24	120

Posttest, page 24

	a	b	c	d
8.	77,106	57,288	744,111	1,981,692
9.	83	185 r4	1,757 r20	1,158
10.	1,899.56	0.4028	$1,551.35	32.4612
11.	130	8,200	720	$0.75
12.	5.208		13.	32

Chapter 2

Pretest, page 25

	a	b	c
1.	$\frac{21}{32}$	$3\frac{3}{8}$	$3\frac{1}{8}$
2.	$12\frac{1}{2}$	$20\frac{4}{5}$	$40\frac{1}{2}$
3.	$13\frac{5}{12}$	$7\frac{1}{5}$	$4\frac{1}{8}$
4.	12	$\frac{4}{15}$	$26\frac{2}{3}$
5.	$\frac{32}{35}$	$\frac{4}{5}$	$\frac{3}{7}$

6.	$\frac{22}{25}$	$2\frac{2}{13}$	$\frac{59}{72}$

Pretest, page 26

7.	$\frac{21}{32}$	9.	$4\frac{3}{8}$	11.	$16\frac{1}{2}$	13.	$\frac{3}{4}$
8.	$3\frac{1}{8}$	10.	$13\frac{1}{8}$	12.	$5\frac{1}{3}$		

Lesson 2.1, page 27

	a	b	c	d
1.	$\frac{4}{15}$	$\frac{5}{8}$	$\frac{5}{8}$	$\frac{3}{10}$
2.	$\frac{7}{16}$	$\frac{16}{27}$	$\frac{3}{10}$	$\frac{9}{35}$
3.	$\frac{1}{9}$	$\frac{11}{18}$	$\frac{4}{25}$	$\frac{9}{28}$
4.	$2\frac{5}{6}$	$4\frac{3}{8}$	$6\frac{33}{40}$	4
5.	$18\frac{2}{15}$	$20\frac{1}{4}$	$7\frac{7}{12}$	$8\frac{3}{4}$
6.	14	$5\frac{4}{9}$	$3\frac{21}{32}$	$3\frac{5}{6}$

Lesson 2.2, page 28

1.	2	2.	4	3.	9

Lesson 2.2, page 29

1.	$\frac{1}{4}$	2.	$\frac{1}{4}$	3.	$\frac{1}{3}$	4.	$\frac{2}{3}$

Lesson 2.3, page 30

	a	b	c	d
1.	$\frac{5}{6}$	$\frac{9}{16}$	$\frac{5}{6}$	$1\frac{1}{15}$
2.	$\frac{4}{7}$	$1\frac{1}{15}$	$2\frac{2}{9}$	$\frac{5}{6}$
3.	$2\frac{5}{8}$	$1\frac{1}{6}$	$\frac{1}{2}$	$2\frac{1}{2}$
4.	$\frac{9}{10}$	$1\frac{1}{27}$	$\frac{4}{5}$	$\frac{6}{7}$

Lesson 2.3, page 31

	a	b	c	d
1.	$2\frac{1}{10}$	$1\frac{1}{2}$	$1\frac{1}{24}$	$8\frac{1}{3}$
2.	$\frac{4}{5}$	$\frac{3}{4}$	$6\frac{6}{7}$	$\frac{1}{2}$
3.	$2\frac{4}{5}$	$\frac{11}{12}$	$1\frac{4}{5}$	$\frac{2}{3}$
4.	$2\frac{11}{12}$	$\frac{1}{12}$	$3\frac{1}{5}$	$\frac{8}{9}$
5.	$2\frac{7}{10}$	$\frac{7}{12}$	$\frac{2}{9}$	$\frac{3}{5}$

Lesson 2.3, page 32

	a	b	c	d
1.	$1\frac{1}{3}$	60	3	$\frac{3}{5}$
2.	$\frac{5}{21}$	$\frac{8}{9}$	$7\frac{1}{2}$	6
3.	$\frac{7}{32}$	$\frac{34}{225}$	$\frac{9}{16}$	$\frac{69}{187}$

4. $\frac{6}{11}$ $\frac{7}{55}$ $\frac{17}{20}$ $\frac{20}{21}$

5. $\frac{11}{15}$ $\frac{1}{3}$ $\frac{42}{55}$ $\frac{17}{24}$

Lesson 2.4, page 33

	a	b	c	d
1.	$\frac{3}{4}$	$\frac{1}{2}$	$2\frac{2}{7}$	$\frac{7}{15}$
2.	$3\frac{6}{7}$	$2\frac{1}{72}$	$\frac{13}{18}$	$\frac{12}{25}$
3.	$2\frac{2}{5}$	$\frac{1}{2}$	$1\frac{1}{3}$	$\frac{17}{24}$
4.	$\frac{9}{10}$	$1\frac{23}{57}$	$\frac{3}{13}$	$5\frac{2}{5}$

Lesson 2.4, page 34

	a	b	c	d
1.	$2\frac{5}{8}$	$5\frac{2}{5}$	$\frac{5}{18}$	$\frac{17}{24}$
2.	$5\frac{1}{2}$	$10\frac{2}{3}$	$\frac{16}{49}$	$2\frac{1}{42}$
3.	$\frac{13}{16}$	$\frac{26}{37}$	$\frac{69}{91}$	$1\frac{1}{15}$
4.	$\frac{112}{155}$	$\frac{130}{171}$	$\frac{39}{74}$	$1\frac{1}{13}$
5.	$1\frac{31}{50}$	$2\frac{18}{19}$	$1\frac{2}{7}$	$4\frac{8}{9}$

Lesson 2.5, page 35

1. $\frac{1}{2}$ **3.** $3\frac{3}{4}$ **5.** 5 **7.** $5\frac{1}{4}$

2. $3\frac{1}{3}$ **4.** $1\frac{1}{3}$ **6.** $2\frac{2}{5}$

Lesson 2.5, page 36

1. $3\frac{1}{16}$ **3.** $\frac{7}{27}$ **5.** 18 **7.** $20\frac{2}{5}$

2. 8 **4.** $17\frac{1}{2}$ **6.** $8\frac{1}{3}$

Posttest, page 37

	a	b	c	d
1.	$\frac{1}{2}$	$\frac{3}{16}$	$\frac{21}{40}$	$\frac{5}{28}$
2.	$3\frac{1}{3}$	$3\frac{1}{2}$	$7\frac{1}{5}$	$4\frac{4}{7}$
3.	$12\frac{1}{2}$	$37\frac{1}{2}$	22	$16\frac{2}{3}$
4.	$8\frac{1}{3}$	$4\frac{1}{2}$	$6\frac{1}{4}$	$11\frac{4}{15}$
5.	$\frac{8}{3}$	$\frac{1}{5}$	$\frac{5}{12}$	$\frac{7}{4}$
6.	$7\frac{1}{2}$	$\frac{4}{25}$	$18\frac{2}{3}$	$\frac{7}{16}$
7.	$\frac{5}{6}$	$1\frac{5}{16}$	$1\frac{11}{21}$	$\frac{5}{9}$
8.	$1\frac{1}{4}$	$1\frac{1}{3}$	1	$\frac{12}{25}$

Posttest, page 38

9. $\frac{5}{18}$ **10.** $3\frac{3}{4}$ **11.** $8\frac{1}{3}$ **12.** $11\frac{2}{3}$

13. $10\frac{5}{6}$ **14.** $1\frac{1}{3}$ **15.** $\frac{4}{5}$

Chapter 3

Pretest, page 39

	a	b	c
1.	$\frac{7}{5} = \frac{28}{20}$	$\frac{4}{6} = \frac{14}{21}$	$\frac{6}{8} = \frac{15}{20}$
2.	$\frac{7}{9} = \frac{14}{18}$	$\frac{15}{18} = \frac{10}{12}$	$\frac{39}{30} = \frac{13}{10}$
3.	$\frac{10}{8} = \frac{30}{24}$	$\frac{11}{12} = \frac{44}{48}$	$\frac{3}{2} = \frac{9}{6}$
4.	$\frac{12}{15} = \frac{4}{5}$	$\frac{10}{14} = \frac{25}{35}$	$\frac{10}{6} = \frac{25}{15}$

	a	b	c	d
5.	0.15	$\frac{3}{20}$	0.22	$\frac{11}{50}$
6.	1.2	$1\frac{1}{5}$	0.54	$\frac{27}{50}$
7.	0.36	$\frac{9}{25}$	2.05	$2\frac{1}{20}$

	a	b	c
8.	12%	1%	40%
9.	406%	12.5%	60%

	a	b
10.	108	45
11.	72	25
12.	24	140
13.	75	140
14.	60.5	205

Pretest, page 40

15. $8   **17.** $3   **19.** 75%   **21.** 184

16. 20   **18.** 9   **20.** 85%   **22.** $11.98

Lesson 3.1, page 41

	a	b			a	b
1.	$\frac{5}{12}$	$\frac{1}{7}$		6.	$\frac{7}{11}$	$\frac{1}{3}$
2.	$\frac{4}{5}$	$\frac{4}{7}$		7.	$\frac{1}{2}$	$\frac{1}{6}$
3.	$\frac{1}{2}$	$\frac{8}{11}$		8.	$\frac{9}{25}$	$\frac{7}{10}$
4.	$\frac{5}{6}$	$\frac{7}{10}$		9.	$\frac{8}{9}$	$\frac{2}{19}$
5.	$\frac{1}{4}$	$\frac{3}{4}$		10.	$\frac{21}{62}$	$\frac{1}{12}$

Lesson 3.1, page 42

	a	b			a	b
1.	$\frac{15}{2}$	$\frac{4}{5}$		4.	$\frac{5}{16}$	$\frac{7}{12}$
2.	$\frac{3}{1}$	$\frac{8}{7}$		5.	$\frac{2}{1}$	$\frac{8}{7}$
3.	$\frac{7}{11}$	$\frac{4}{5}$		6.	$\frac{3}{5}$	$\frac{3}{2}$

Lesson 3.2, page 43

	a	b	c
1.	8	16	1

2.	9	1	10
3.	21	2	21
4.	64	11	15
5.	15	36	10

Lesson 3.2, page 44

	a	b	c
1.	1	9	8
2.	4	16	5
3.	8	6	6
4.	49	5	10
5.	70	9	10

Lesson 3.3, page 45

1. Cans, 4, 8, 12; Cost, $2.25, $4.50, $6.75
2. Ice Cream, 180, 360, 540, 720, 900, 1,080; Hours, 2, 4, 6, 8, 10, 12
3. Distance, 650, 1300, 1950; Hours, 3, 6, 9
4. Bagels, 640, 1280, 1920, 2560; Hours, 4, 8, 12, 16

Lesson 3.4, page 46

1. 5   3. 24 minutes   5. 12
2. $\frac{1}{2}$ hour   4. $\frac{1}{2}$ day   6. $130

Lesson 3.5, page 47

1. 1,320; 22 miles per gallon   4. Village Market
2. 720; 480 quarts per day   5. Quick Stop
3. 1,180; 118 miles per hour   6. 440; 220 people per hour

Lesson 3.5, page 48

1. Keith   3. Nicole   5. Mrs. Jimenez's class
2. Carl   4. Music Land   6. $28

Lesson 3.6, page 49

	Fraction	Decimal			Fraction	Decimal
1.	$\frac{1}{50}$	0.02		8.	$\frac{11}{100}$	0.11
2.	$\frac{2}{25}$	0.08		9.	$\frac{3}{100}$	0.03
3.	$\frac{27}{100}$	0.27		10.	$\frac{11}{50}$	0.22
4.	$\frac{13}{100}$	0.13		11.	$\frac{17}{100}$	0.17
5.	$\frac{17}{25}$	0.68		12.	$\frac{83}{100}$	0.83
6.	$\frac{18}{25}$	0.72		13.	$\frac{97}{100}$	0.97
7.	$\frac{14}{25}$	0.56		14.	$\frac{43}{100}$	0.43

Lesson 3.6, page 50

	Fraction	Decimal			Fraction	Decimal
1.	$\frac{7}{100}$	0.07		8.	$\frac{39}{100}$	0.39
2.	$\frac{13}{100}$	0.13		9.	$\frac{1}{10}$	0.10
3.	$\frac{12}{25}$	0.48		10.	$\frac{31}{50}$	0.62
4.	$\frac{71}{100}$	0.71		11.	$\frac{3}{4}$	0.75
5.	$\frac{27}{100}$	0.27		12.	$\frac{97}{100}$	0.97

6.	$\frac{1}{50}$	0.02		13.	$\frac{53}{100}$	0.53
7.	$\frac{3}{20}$	0.15		14.	$\frac{41}{50}$	0.82

Lesson 3.7, page 51

	a	b			a	b
1.	$5\frac{1}{5}$	76		7.	$31\frac{1}{2}$	$8\frac{1}{10}$
2.	$9\frac{3}{5}$	7		8.	$3\frac{17}{25}$	$14\frac{2}{5}$
3.	18	$7\frac{1}{2}$		9.	54	$21\frac{1}{2}$
4.	$1\frac{24}{25}$	$3\frac{4}{5}$		10.	$4\frac{4}{5}$	$5\frac{2}{5}$
5.	8	$6\frac{3}{4}$		11.	36	19
6.	64	15		12.	$10\frac{1}{2}$	$\frac{3}{4}$

Lesson 3.8, page 52

	a	b			a	b
1.	20.48	10.4		7.	5.88	38
2.	2.225	4.62		8.	9	31.24
3.	6.96	20		9.	5.796	64
4.	6.132	42.14		10.	7.84	27.9
5.	2.048	3.19		11.	2.56	24
6.	42	4.5		12.	4.32	2.7

Lesson 3.9, page 53

	a	b			a	b
1.	60%	20%		6.	20%	150%
2.	15%	64%		7.	30%	200%
3.	15%	40%		8.	37.5%	125%
4.	10%	90%		9.	50%	25%
5.	75%	40%		10.	120%	80%

Lesson 3.10, page 54

1. $48.65   3. 18   5. $90
2. $194.60   4. 480   6. 375

Lesson 3.10, page 55

1. 17%   3. 15%   5. 18%   7. 4.8
2. $35.75   4. 1,150   6. 69   8. 280

Posttest, page 56

	a	b	c	d
1.	15	27	3	
2.	5	6	21	
3.	6	16	15	
4.	14	9	4	
5.	0.24	$\frac{6}{25}$	1.10	$1\frac{1}{10}$
6.	0.37	$\frac{37}{100}$	0.55	$\frac{11}{20}$
7.	0.06	$\frac{3}{50}$	2.35	$2\frac{7}{20}$
8.	16%	5%	60%	
9.	80%	87.5%	130%	
10.	80	84%		
11.	15	160		
12.	5%	27.2		

| 13. | 72 | 12.5% |
| 14. | 60 | 4.4 |

Posttest, page 57

| 15. | 4 | **17.** | 6 | **19.** | 60% | **21.** | $4,375.00 |
| 16. | $45 | **18.** | $24 | **20.** | $\frac{11}{20}$ | **22.** | 42 |

Chapter 4

Pretest, page 58

	a	b	
1.	−8	1	
2.	−5	−35	
3.	21	16	

	a	b	c
4.	3	10	5
5.	9	23	7
6.	13	5	1
7.	<	>	>
8.	<	<	>
9.	>	>	<

	a	b
10.	−89, −26, 8, 42	−90, −84, −57, 91
11.	−81, −5, 20, 87	53, 55, 73, 89
12.	−91, −46, 12, 52	−38, −23, 22, 41

Pretest, page 59

13.	(7, 6)	**16.**	(5, −8)	**19.**	F
14.	(−8, 8)	**17.**	H	**20.**	B
15.	(−6, −3)	**18.**	D	**21-24.**	Check graph.

Lesson 4.1, page 60

	a	b
1.		
2.		
3.		
4.		
5.		
6.		
7.	−10	−1
8.	3	−7
9.	4	8
10.	−13	15
11.	32	−27
12.	−17	20

Lesson 4.2, page 61

	a	b			a	b
1.	−45	8	**7.**		−10	7
2.	528	62	**8.**		60	−95
3.	345	−8	**9.**		−97	−34
4.	7500	−80	**10.**		−100	15
5.	10	−250	**11.**		−25	390
6.	3	−8	**12.**		95	6,000

Lesson 4.3, page 62

	a	b	c
1.	4	13	−10
2.	−7	11	2
3.	−12	−5	1
4.	14	−8	−13
5.	3	7	−4
6.	−15	9	12
7.	16	6	−20
8.	−40	−24	17
9.	33	−41	19
10.	26	18	−35
11.	−53	21	30
12.	25	−21	47

Lesson 4.3, page 63

	a	b	c
1.	64	81	−32
2.	−8	19	53
3.	−76	-3	11
4.	62	-95	−42
5.	2	36	−9
6.	−13	48	27
7.	35	29	−23
8.	−51	57	80
9.	73	−55	46
10.	65	37	−59
11.	67	70	50
12.	34	−63	71
13.	58	93	21
14.	−6	−17	−88
15.	10	49	−5
16.	−22	−79	31

Lesson 4.4, page 64

	a	b	c
1.	−2	−7	1
2.	6	3	−5
3.	2 < 7	−1 > −4	5 > 0
4.	−4 < 1	0 > −8	−8 > −10
5.	7 > −7	−2 < 0	4 < 6
6.	1 > −1	6 > 3	−6 < −3
7.	4 > −2	−6 < −4	3 > −3
8.	−5, −3, 0	−8, 2, 8	
9.	−7, −3, 0, 5	−2, −1, 2, 4	
10.	−6, −3, −2, 2, 5	−8, −3, −2, 0, 5	

Lesson 4.4, page 65

	a	b	c
1.	66 > 3	43 < 83	−24 < 82
2.	99 > 84	−33 > −90	−37 = −37
3.	28 > 7	−24 < 61	−36 > −88
4.	−27 > −52	−49 > −69	42 < 98
5.	88 > −99	47 > −44	−8 > −45
6.	46 > −26	13 > −1	39 < 51
7.	8 > −18	61 > −70	−4 < −1
8.	−12 > −14	−1 < 0	57 > −73

	a	b
9.	−37, 16, 51, 61	−86, −49, 21, 90
10.	−84, −67, −65, 10	−97, −78, −62, 11

Grade 6 Answers

11.	−37, −35, 48, 81		−68, −9, 19, 95
12.	−37, 9, 51, 61		−49, 15, 21, 90
13.	−11, −4, 9, 14		−75, −23, 27, 74
14.	−80, −79, 2, 81		−47, −39, 47, 93

Lesson 4.4, page 66

	a	b	c
1.	92 > 35	−56 > −57	−77 < 37
2.	78 > −96	−99 < −94	34 > −60
3.	−1 > −37	6 > −78	34 > −43
4.	4 > −4	−66 < −13	−66 < −45
5.	−10 < 51	76 > 13	−69 > −79
6.	18 < 80	−12 > −81	−61 < 57
7.	33 > −64	17 > 13	−21 < 19
8.	18 < 80	−12 > −81	−61 < 57

	a	b
9.	−67, −65, 10, 20	−97, −78, −57, 11
10.	−39, −37, 48, 81	−96, −9, 19, 95
11.	9, 47, 51, 61	−49, 15, 22, 90
12.	−65, 10, 20, 55	−97, −78, −68, −57
13.	−34, −16, 0, 14	−12, −7, 67, 72
14.	−46, −2, 46, 52	−92, −52, −28, −3

Lesson 4.5, page 67

1.	(−7, 8)	4.	(2, −2)	7.	I	10.	D
2.	(3, 9)	5.	(−9, −6)	8.	K		
3.	(−4, −4)	6.	J	9.	F		

Lesson 4.5, page 68

1.	(0, 4)	5.	(−3, −3)	9.	S	13.	R
2.	(−8, 3)	6.	(5, 7)	10.	Q	14.	W
3.	(−6, −6)	7.	(−2, 7)	11.	V	15.	T
4.	(7, 0)	8.	(4, −5)	12.	X	16.	U

Lesson 4.6, page 69

1. 11 2. 15 3. 15 4. 12 5. 4

Posttest, page 70

	a	b
1.	9	−17
2.	−22	41
3.	5	−76

	a	b	c
4.	3	−10	45
5.	−29	12	8
6.	26	2	-18
7.	92 > 79	50 > −76	−74 < −35
8.	−77 < 15	−11 > −49	−14 > −73
9.	−18 > −76	44 < 72	−45 < −12

	a	b
10.	−70, −28, 60, 86	−54, −38, −17, 45
11.	−97, −71, −63, 36	−36, 26, 60, 63
12.	38, 48, 56, 89	−47, 49, 78, 97

Posttest, page 71

13.	(−9, −5)	16.	(−7, 5)	19.	N	25.	17
14.	(3, −6)	17.	P	20.	R	26.	14
15.	(1, 7)	18.	T	21–24.	Check graph.		

Mid-Test

Mid-test, page 72

	a	b	c	d	e
1.	5,593	93,993	24,624	1,802,340	2,562,648

2.	12 r8	7,809	137 r43	2,581 r10	428
3.	55.68	0.32226	$1350.40	$114.4836	165.78
4.	75	665	75.6	2476	392
5.	$\frac{1}{2}$	$\frac{35}{48}$	$3\frac{3}{4}$	$9\frac{1}{3}$	14
6.	30	$\frac{3}{20}$	$1\frac{5}{16}$	$\frac{13}{15}$	$1\frac{7}{8}$

Mid-test, page 73

	a	b	c
7.	4	35	15
8.	28	18	24
9.	11	2	8

10. 42   11. 213   12. Shop and Save

13.	15%	80%	28%
14.	0.3	0.7225	3.46
15.	$\frac{3}{4}$	$\frac{1}{5}$	$1\frac{2}{5}$

Mid-test, page 74

	a	b	c
16.	2.7	1.2	19.8
17.	82	3	80
18.	25	4	95
19.	7	71	−68
20.	100	−25	95
21.	−37	68	−25
22.	−32 > −35	−68 < −41	40 > 27
23.	96 > 17	20 < 36	20 < 48
24.	72 > −15	−29 < 62	14 > −77

	a	b
25.	−85, −56, −6, 6	−82, −47, −3, 80
26.	−60, 5, 10, 99	37, 66, 73, 76
27.	−47, −37, −7, 16	−56, 61, 75, 97

Mid-test, page 75

28.	(3, 9)	31.	(−3, 2)	34.	D	40.	21
29.	(2, −3)	32.	H	35.	B	41.	16
30.	(−1, 7)	33.	F	36–39.	Check graph.		

Chapter 5

Pretest, page 76

	a	b	c
1.	2 × 2 × 2 × 2	9 × 9	5 × 5 × 5
2.	4 × 4	8 × 8 × 8 × 8 × 8	7 × 7 × 7
3.	4^4	2^3	6^5
4.	3^8	9^3	8^6
5.	expression	equation	expression
6.	equation	expression	expression
7.	C = 5, V = y	C = 2, V = x	C = 1, V = n
8.	C = 12, V = z	C = 4, V = m	C = 9, V = d
9.	4 × (8 − 3)	13.	6 × (2 − 1)
10.	4 + 5 × 3	14.	3 × (40 ÷ 8)
11.	16 − (4 × 2)	15.	7 − (4 × 2)
12.	25 ÷ (5 + 3)		

Pretest, page 77

	a	b	c
16.	8	2	2
17.	11	0	0
18.	7	16	10

19. 16   1   25

20. $1\frac{1}{2}$ 36   3

21. 100   5   9

22. $3s = 48$; $16; $16, $32

23. the number of men; $23 - n = 5$ or $n + 5 = 23$; 18; 18

Lesson 5.1, page 78

	a	b	c
1.	3×10^1	4×10^3	5×10^4
2.	6×10^5	7×10^2	9×10^1
3.	4×10^4	1×10^5	4×10^2
4.	$3 \times 3 \times 3$	$5 \times 5 \times 5 \times 5$	$1 \times 1 \times 1 \times 1 \times 1$
5.	12×12	$8 \times 8 \times 8$	$6 \times 6 \times 6$
6.	$7 \times 7 \times 7 \times 7$	$4 \times 4 \times 4 \times 4$	$11 \times 11 \times 11 \times 11$
7.	3^3	8^2	7^5
8.	24^2	4^3	6^6
9.	2^4	38^3	5^5
10.	16	64	1
11.	64	81	125
12.	243	216	121

Lesson 5.1, page 79

	a	b	c
1.	$3 \times 3 \times 3 \times 3 \times 3$	$9 \times 9 \times 9$	$2 \times 2 \times 2 \times 2 \times 2 \times 2 \times 2$
2.	10×10	$3 \times 3 \times 3 \times 3$	$2 \times 2 \times 2 \times 2 \times 2 \times 2 \times 2 \times 2$
3.	$7 \times 7 \times 7$	4×4	7×7
4.	$9 \times 9 \times 9$	8	12×12
5.	$5 \times 5 \times 5 \times 5$	$11 \times 11 \times 11$	$6 \times 6 \times 6 \times 6 \times 6$
6.	$4 \times 4 \times 4 \times 4$	$10 \times 10 \times 10$	$8 \times 8 \times 8 \times 8 \times 8 \times 8$
7.	3^3	5^5	2^6
8.	9^3	4^7	21^2
9.	10^4	8^5	7^4
10.	32,768	256	81
11.	36	9	10,000
12.	256	2,401	144

Lesson 5.2, page 80

	a	b	c
1.	expression	equation	expression
2.	equation	expression	equation
3.	3; x	4; y	
4.	1; z	5; n	
5.	7; b	1; m	
6.	1; r	6; d	
7.	$n + 5$	$8 - x$	
8.	$x + 7$	$n \times 11$	
9.	$6n = 18$	$70 - n = 29$	
10.	$\frac{8}{n} = 2$	$7 \times 12 = 84$	

11. six decreased by a number is equal to three

12. the product of five and thirteen is equal to 65

Lesson 5.2, page 81

	a	b	c
1.	expression	equation	equation
2.	expression	equation	expression
3.	expression	equation	expression
4.	equation	expression	expression
5.	$C = 6, V = g$	$C = 1, V = p$	
6.	$C = 5, V = r$	$C = 9, V = t$	
7.	$C = 2, V = x$	$C = 4, V = n$	

8. $C = 3, V = a$ $C = 7, V = d$

9. $C = 20, V = s$ $C = 1, V = j$

10. $3 + b$ $8 \times (f + 7)$

11. $8 \times d$ $p + 4 = 9$

12. $(4 \times m) - 3$ $r - 2 = 8$

13. $4 \times (5 + x)$ 10×2

14. $12 \times r - 7$ $9 + k$

Lesson 5.3, page 82

	a	b
1.	$x + 5$	$12 \div n$
2.	$7n$ or $7 \times n$	$7 - c$
3.	$n + 15 = 23$	$x \div 4$ or $\frac{1}{4}x$
4.	$6 + p$	$15m$ or $15 \times m$
5.	$11 - n = 7$	**8.** a number decreased by 5
6.	$8n + 4 = 84$	**9.** three times a number divided by 6
7.	$n \div 5 = 6$	

Lesson 5.3, page 83

	a	b
1.	$(3 \times d) - 8$	$x - 3$
2.	$g - 2 = 14$	$z + 8$
3.	$7 + z$	$(4 \times d) - 2$
4.	$\frac{2}{5} \times (6 + s)$	$9 - c$
5.	$10 - x$	$4f - 9$
6.	$5a - 3$	$y - 3 = 15$
7.	$9 + s$	$8 + t$
8.	$h - 9$	$\frac{1}{3}(7 + k)$

9. 9 divided by x

10. the product of 3 and a number is 27

11. the product of 6 and a number decreased by 4

12. half of a number increased by 9 is 11

13. 14 divided a number

14. the product of 6 and a number is 42

15. the product of 9 and a number decreased by 10

16. one-fourth a number increased by 8 is 16

Lesson 5.4, page 84

1.	$28z + 56b$	9.	$30a + 54b$
2.	$16x + 72$	10.	$27x + 5,625$
3.	$4 \times 4r$	11.	$7(3c)$
4.	$27 + 72x$	12.	$18 + 63f$
5.	$48 + 96t$	13.	$67,228g - 134,456d$
6.	$\frac{3t}{4}$	14.	$\frac{3e}{5}$
7.	$8s^3 + 4$	15.	$15z^6 + 15$
8.	$90x + 120$	16.	$10y + 20$

Lesson 5.4, page 85

1.	$4a + 4b$	9.	$6c - 6f$
2.	$27a + 24b$	10.	$40b - 40c$
3.	$9x + 18y$	11.	$8g - 24d$
4.	$18x + 18$	12.	$21h + 48$
5.	$250 + 500c$	13.	$3,072 + 5,120t$
6.	$\frac{2x}{3}$	14.	$\frac{2d}{10}$ or $\frac{d}{5}$
7.	$192 + 80c$	15.	$32,400 + 1,296t$
8.	$238r + 459 - 7r$ or $231r + 459$	16.	$(380f - 19w^4) + 3f$ or $383f - 19w^4$

Grade 6 Answers

Lesson 5.5, page 86

	a	b	c
1.	addition	subtraction	
2.	subtraction	addition	
3.	6	4	17
4.	11	12	0
5.	12	10	0
6.	3	21	9
7.	0	20	4
8.	30	15	10

9. $x + \$6 = \$20$; $x = \$14$
10. $g + 12 = 27$; $g = 15$

Lesson 5.5, page 87

	a	b	c
1.	7	6	15
2.	14	2	22
3.	33	13	0
4.	23	0	15
5.	14	24	1
6.	6	6	24

7. $21 + n = 37$; 16
8. $n - 9 = 33$; 42
9. $2 + 5 + n = 25$; 18

Lesson 5.6, page 88

	a	b	c
1.	divide	multiply	
2.	multiply	divide	
3.	3	25	12
4.	9	1	8
5.	2	16	5
6.	3	$2\frac{1}{2}$	10
7.	$\frac{1}{4}$	20	81
8.	2	40	3
9.	36	6	10
10.	40	16	1
11.	6	150	3
12.	4	4	8

Lesson 5.6, page 89

	a	b	c
1.	9	5	6
2.	12	27	15
3.	8	1	6
4.	50	36	48
5.	5	0	16
6.	19	28	63

7. $6 \times n = 12$ or $12 \div 6 = n$; 2
8. $48 \div n = 12$ or $48 \div 12 = n$; 4
9. $25 \times n = 150$ or $150 \div 25 = n$; 6

Lesson 5.7, page 90

1. the number of Jaden's cards; $n - 35 = 52$; 87
2. the number of tickets; $\$6.95 \times n = \$55.60$; 8
3. the width of the room; $1.5 \times n = 18$; 12
4. the Grizzlies' score; $n + 11 = 92$; 81

Lesson 5.7, page 91

1. the cost of candy bars; $\$3 + (\$4 \times c) = \$11$; \$2
2. the number of students on each bus; $(6 \times s) + 8 = 248$; 40

3. the number of comic books Todd had; $c \div 2 + 6 = 16$; 20
4. how many hours Mike had the bike; $\$12 + (\$6 \times h) = \$48$; 6
5. Susan's weekly allowance; $a - \$8 + \$5 = \$20$; \$23

Lesson 5.8, page 92

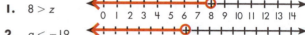

1. $8 > z$
2. $g < -19$
3. $d < 12$
4. $13 > k$
5. $x > -17$
6. $y < -17$
7. $0 \leq r$
8. $w \geq 3$

Lesson 5.8, page 93

1. $x < 14$
2. $y > 18$
3. $p < -15$
4. $v < -10$
5. $s \geq -12$
6. $f \geq 6$
7. $w < -9$
8. $g \leq 12$

Lesson 5.9, page 94

1. total cost $= \$1.25 \times$ weight

Dependent Variable	Cost (Dollars)	\$1.25	\$2.50	\$3.75
Independent Variable	Weight (Pounds)	1	2	3

2. height $= 6 + (2 \times$ time$)$

Dependent Variable	Height (Feet)	12	18	54
Independent Variable	Time (Months)	3	6	24

Lesson 5.9, page 95

1. time $= 150 \div$ reading speed

Dependent Variable	Time	10	7.5	5
Independent Variable	Speed (pgs./day)	15	20	30

2. height $= 12 - ($time $\times 2)$

Dependent Variable	Height (Inches)	10	8	6
Independent Variable	Time (Hours)	1	2	3

3. height $= 1 + 1.5($time$)$

Dependent Variable	Height (Inches)	2.5	4	5.5

Grade 6 Answers

Independent Variable	Time (Days)	1	2	3

4. temperature = 250° + (8° × time)

Dependent Variable	Temperature (°F)	258	266	274
Independent Variable	Time (Minutes)	1	2	3

Posttest, page 96

	a	b	c
1.	3×3×3×3×3	12×12	6×6×6×6
2.	5×5×5×5	7×7×7	8×8×8×8×8×8
3.	4×4×4×4×4	2×2×2×2×2×2×2×2	9×9×9
4.	2^5	8^3	25^2
5.	4^3	5^8	15^3
6.	expression	equation	expression
7.	equation	expression	expression
8.	C = 9, V = y	C = 4, V = b	C = 1, V = m
9.	2 × (7 − 3)	**13.**	(7 × 2) ÷ 3
10.	3 + (4 × 2)	**14.**	2 × (45 ÷ 9)
11.	12 − (4 × 3)	**15.**	15 − (4 × 2)
12.	(20 ÷ 5) + 16	**16.**	(16 + 9) × 3

Posttest, page 97

	a	b	c
17.	8	3	4
18.	27	16	0
19.	7	0	6
20.	9	1	2
21.	$1\frac{1}{2}$	9	$1\frac{1}{2}$
22.	16	1	6

23. the number of video games; $72.60 ÷ $24.20 = g ; 3

24. 2n − 4 = 130; 67; 63

Chapter 6

Pretest, page 98

	a	b	c
1.	240 sq. in.	$187\frac{1}{2}$ sq. ft.	77 sq. cm
2.	6.12 sq. m	1,376 sq. m	235.45 sq. cm
3.	1,200 cu. cm	960 cu. ft.	$\frac{16}{125}$ cu. m

Pretest, page 99

	a	b
4.	(−3, −3)	(−5, −3) or (4, 2)

5. 165 sq. ft.　**6.** 300 cu. in.　**7.** 54 sq. ft.

Lesson 6.1, page 100

	a	b
1.	40 sq. in.	$27\frac{1}{2}$ sq. ft.
2.	$12\frac{1}{2}$ sq. ft.	36 sq. yd.

Lesson 6.1, page 101

	a	b	c
1.	27.5 sq. ft.	48 sq. yd.	104.5 sq. in.
2.	10 sq. ft.	123.25 sq. cm	32 sq. m

Lesson 6.2, page 102

	a	b	c
1.	18 sq. yd.	324 sq. m	276 sq. cm
2.	216 sq. km	529 sq. in.	48 sq. ft.
3.	9 in.	13 ft.	9 m

Lesson 6.2, page 103

	a	b	c
1.	624	450	651
2.	306	157.5	137.5

Lesson 6.3, page 104

	a	b	c
1.	80	56	26
2.	57	20	28

Lesson 6.3, page 105

	a	b	c
1.	52 sq. ft.	48 sq. m	24 sq. cm
2.	185 sq. yd.	12 sq. mi.	20 sq. in.

Lesson 6.4, page 106

	a	b	c
1.	420 cu. yd.	512 cu. in.	12,000 cu. ft.
2.	336 cu. ft.	100 cu. in.	648 cu. in.

Lesson 6.4, page 107

	a	b	c
1.	576 cu. cm	1,728 cu. cm	2,112 cu. m
2.	144 cu. mm	1,620 cu. mm	3,600 cu. cm
3.	1,280 cu. mm	12,000 cu. cm	7,800 cu. mm

Lesson 6.4, page 108

	a	b		a	b
1.	$\frac{30}{343}$ cu. in.	$\frac{4}{243}$ cu. ft.	2.	$\frac{160}{729}$ cu. cm	$\frac{40}{1331}$ cu. ft.

Lesson 6.5, page 109

1. 54 cu. in.　**3.** 480 sq. yd.　**5.** 375 sq. in.
2. 1,440 cu. in.　**4.** 36 cu. in.　**6.** 3,600 sq. yd.

Lesson 6.5, page 110

1. 500 sq. m　**3.** 1,260 sq. cm　**5.** 3,000 cu. cm
2. 0.102 cu. m　**4.** 87.72 sq. m　**6.** 168 sq. cm

Lesson 6.6, page 111

	a	b	c
1.	862	144	1,720
2.	90	1,710	1,270

Lesson 6.6, page 112

	a	b	c
1.	62 sq. in.	48.7 sq. ft.	172 sq. yd.
2.	856 sq. cm	104 sq. m	248 sq. in.
3.	85.5 sq. ft.	2970 sq. mm	81.44 sq. cm

Lesson 6.7, page 113

	a	b	c
1.	240	540	217
2.	459	260	1254

Lesson 6.8, page 114

1. (0, 4)　**2.** (−2, −4)

Lesson 6.9, page 115

1. (3, 6) or (−5, 2)　**2.** (−4, 2) or (5, −6)

Grade 6 Answers

Posttest, page 116

	a	b	c
1.	392 sq. cm	315 sq. in.	72 sq. in.
2.	65.55 sq. in.	334 sq. m	644 sq. m
3.	3,360 cu. m	192 cu. mm	1,200 cu. cm

Posttest, page 117

	a	b
4.	(−2, −4)	Answers may vary but could include (−1, 5) or (2, −3)
5.	216	**6.** 2,400	**7.** 5,040 cu. in.; 3.125 cu. ft.

Chapter 7

Pretest, page 118

	a	b
1.	yes	no
2.	no	yes
3.	10	
4.	week 5	

5. Angelica
6. 5 miles

7.
Stem	Leaves
1	8
2	4, 5
3	1, 6
5	6
7	2

8.
Stem	Leaves
1	5, 6
2	1, 3, 3, 6, 6
3	0, 2
4	1

Pretest, page 119

9. mean-80; median-82; mode-66; range-32
10. mean-12; median-12; mode-12, range-14
11. 60–80   **13.** 11   **15.** 51
12. 0–20   **14.** 29   **16.** more

Lesson 7.1, page 120

	a	b			a	b
1.	statistical	not		4.	not	statistical
2.	statistical	statistical		5.	not	statistical
3.	not	not				

Lesson 7.1, page 121

Answers may vary.
1. How tall are the students in my school?
2. What scores did students score on the last spelling test?
3. How many pages are in the typical 6th grade novel?
4. How many students are in PE classes at my school?
5. How much do average apples cost?
6. What is the most popular car in the U.S.?
7. How many minutes do children exercise per week?

Lesson 7.2, page 122

Answers may vary.
1a. The data spreads over 7 points.
1b. The center value of the data is 67.
1c. The lowest value in the data is 62.
2a. Some values in the data set are equal to 0.
2b. The highest value in the data set is 100.
2c. 0 appears the most in the data set.
3a. The data spreads across 92 points.
3b. 45 appears the most frequently in the data set.
3c. 45 is the middle value in the data set.

Lesson 7.2, page 123

Answers may vary.
1a. The data spreads over 1.9 points.
1b. The center value of the data is 6.4.
1c. The lowest value in the data is 5.4.
2a. Some values in the data set are greater than 0.
2b. The highest value in the data set is 9.
2c. 5 appears the most frequently in the data set.
3a. The data spreads across 7 points.
3b. 3 appears the most frequently in the data set.
3c. 4 is the middle value in the data set.

Lesson 7.3, page 124

	a	b			a	b
1.	60	78		4.	62	78
2.	106	98		5.	108	83
3.	111	92		6.	70.5	49.5

Lesson 7.4, page 125

	a	b			a	b
1.	34	19		4.	32	19
2.	19	2		5.	5	77
3.	34	6		6.	78	36

Lesson 7.5, page 126

	a	b			a	b
1.	4	40		4.	277	21
2.	28	108		5.	73	4
3.	26	24		6.	14 and 93	32

Lesson 7.6, page 127

	a	b			a	b
1.	$35\frac{3}{5}$	14		3.	68	51
	35	12			71	49
	43	12			79	37
2.	13	$20\frac{1}{6}$				
	12	$18\frac{1}{2}$				
	12	15				

Lesson 7.7, page 128

	a	b			a	b
1.	median	mean		3.	median	mean
2.	mean	mode		4.	median	mode

Lesson 7.7, page 129

	a	b
1.	mean	84; 84; 80
2.	median	72.75; 78; 77.5
3.	mean	114.57; 115; no mode
4.	median	$23.57; $21; $21

Lesson 7.8, page 130

	a	b			a	b
1.	3	5		4.	11	6
2.	10	10		5.	7	9
3.	8	4				

Lesson 7.9, page 131

	a	b
1.	5; 2; 7; 5	85; 75; 92.5; 17.5
2.	90; 72.5; 97.5; 25	12; 5; 43; 38

Grade 6 Answers

3. 16.5; 4; 39; 35   29; 16; 64; 48

Lesson 7.10, page 132
1a. 15.29; 5.29, 5.29,0.29,0.29, 0.71, 2.71, 7.71; 3.18
1b. 48.29; 10.29, 7.29, 3.29, 2.71, 3.71, 6.71, 7.71; 5.96
2a. 17.57; 7.57, 6.57, 5.57, 0.43, 4.43, 7.43, 7.43; 5.63
2b. 45.1; 34.1, 23.1, 23.1, 12.1, 1.1, 9.9, 9.9, 9.9, 20.9, 42.9; 18.7

Lesson 7.11, page 133
1. 37; 16.5; 9   **3.** 76; 37; 19.1   **5.** 62; 16; 13.08
2. 35; 14; 8   **4.** 8; 4; 2.04   **6.** 42; 23; 12

Lesson 7.12, page 134

1.

Stem	Leaves
1	3 4
2	1 8
3	1 3 4

Stem	Leaves
3	8 9
4	9
5	0 4 7
6	3 4
7	2 9

2.

Stem	Leaves
2	5 7
3	4 7 8
4	8 9

Stem	Leaves
7	3 5
8	1 4 7 8
9	1 3 6 9

3.

Stem	Leaves
1	3 7 9
2	4 5
3	3 8

Stem	Leaves
2	3 5 6 7
3	3 5 7
4	1 5 6

Lesson 7.13, page 135
1. 75   **3.** 50   **5.** 15
2. 9   **4.** 20   **6.** 30
7.

Lesson 7.14, page 136
1. Lopez   **5.** 55   **9.** 105
2. 30   **6.** Wed.   **10.** 195
3. Wed.   **7.** Thurs.
4. Martin   **8.** Tues.

Lesson 7.15, page 137
1. 1,800   **7.** 35
2. 25–30   **8.** Answers will vary but may include
3. 0–5   300 to 400 trees.
4. 34.7%   **9.** Answers will vary.
5. 65.3%   **10.** Students should draw a star above
6. 50   the 20–25 feet bar.

Lesson 7.16, page 138
1. mode-85; median-84; mean-82.44; range-66; IQR-15; MAD-9.79

Stem	Leaves
3	4
6	3
7	2 8 9
8	1 2 3 3 5 5 5 8
9	4 6 7 9
10	0

85 is the value that appears most frequently in the data set. 34 is the lowest value in the set and makes the mean lower. Therefore, the best measure of center to describe the data set is the median, 84.

2. mode-3; median-3; mean-3.2; range-4; IQR-2; MAD-1.04

Stem	Leaves
0	1 2 3 3 3 4 4 5 5

All of the values in this data set are single digits. The range is only 5, so the mean, 3.2, is the best measure of center to describe this data set.

Lesson 7.16, page 139
1. mode-64; median-57; mean-57.83; range-20; IQR-11; MAD-5.17

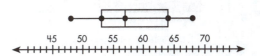

This data set has a range of 20 and is evenly distributed. The mean, 57.83, is the best measure of center to describe the set.

2. mode-45; median-45; mean-40; range-60; IQR-15; MAD-14

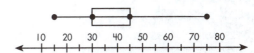

The median and mode of this data set, 45, greatly affects the way the distribution looks. Most of the data points fall either below or along the median.

Lesson 7.16, page 140

mode-15 & 20; median-20; mean-19.17; range-35; IQR-12.5; MAD-7.64

Number of Notebooks Sold

This data set has is evenly distributed in the middle, but has outliers on the low end. Therefore, the median, 20, is the best measure of center to use to describe the data set.

Grade 6 Answers

Posttest, page 141

1. What is the age of teachers in my school?
2. How much money from their allowances do my classmates save?
3.
Stem	Leaves
1	2 8
2	2 2 5
3	1 6 8

4.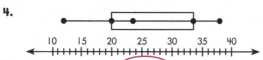

5. mode-13; median-13; mean-13; range-14; IQR-6; MAD-2.86

Posttest, page 142

6. mode-47; median-45; mean-44; range-21; IQR-11; MAD-5.56

7.

Car Gas Mileage

8. 5   9. 5   10. 15–20

Final Test

Final Test, page 143

	a	b	c	d
1.	7,936	94,176	6.052	24.6015
2.	228 r10	2695 r5	4.31	2.72
3.	$\frac{3}{40}$	$\frac{2}{7}$	$1\frac{27}{28}$	$3\frac{19}{24}$
4.	$1\frac{5}{7}$	$\frac{6}{7}$	$1\frac{7}{8}$	$2\frac{7}{9}$
5.	.25	$\frac{1}{4}$	44%	$\frac{11}{25}$
6.	1.1	$1\frac{1}{10}$	98%	$\frac{49}{50}$
7.	.73	$\frac{73}{100}$	65%	$\frac{13}{20}$

	a	b	c
8.	$\frac{3}{5} = \frac{12}{20}$	$\frac{4}{6} = \frac{12}{18}$	$\frac{4}{8} = \frac{10}{20}$
9.	$\frac{5}{8} = \frac{15}{24}$	$\frac{8}{25} = \frac{32}{100}$	$\frac{12}{36} = \frac{1}{3}$

Final Test, page 144

10a.	$-12 > 30$	10d.	$-29 > -45$
10b.	$82 > 17$	10e.	$-57 < 15$
10c.	$-21 > -57$	10f.	$15 > -69$

	a	b	c
11.	$4 \times 4 =$	$15 \times 15 \times 15 =$	$2 \times 2 \times 2 \times 2 \times 2 \times 2 =$
12.	5^3	6^5	12^4

13. $24 \div (8 - 4)$ 14. $6 + (4 \times 7)$ 15-19. Check graph.
20. 9 units   21. 14 units   22. 25 units

Final Test, page 145

	a	b	c
23.	$(3 \times 4) + (3 \times 2)$	$2 \times (5 - 3)$	
24.	$6 \times (8 + 4)$	$(8 \times 7) - (8 \times 4)$	
25.	$17 < c$	$d > 4$	$19 = a$
26.	$b = 6$	$p = 18$	$n = 40$

27. $time = \dfrac{10}{speed}$

Dependent Variable	Time (Hours)	2.5	1	.25
Independent Variable	Speed (mph)	4	10	40

28. (4, 1)   29. $(4, -4)$ or $(10, 0)$

Final Test, page 146

	a	b	c
30.	494 sq. cm	405 sq. in.	10,800 cu. ft.
31.	126 sq. cm	324 sq. mm	176 sq. ft.
32.	812 sq. in.	60 cu. m	182 sq. cm
33.	80 sq. mm	198.75 sq. ft.	25 sq. ft.

Final Test, page 147

34.
Stem	Leaves
0	8 9 9
1	0 1 2 3 4 5 6 7 7 8
2	0 1 2 2 2 3 3

35.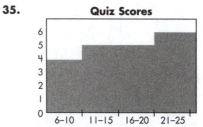

Quiz Scores

36. mean = 16.1; median = 16.5; mode = 22; range = 15; IQR = 10; MAD = 4.4
37. 25%   38. 23   39. 8   40. 30%